To Joe,
from Sadi.

I hope you enjoy the "story of Spitfire P8074

THE STORY OF THE DONEGAL SPITFIRE

Best Wishes

Jonny McNee

Dec 2013

Jonny McNee

Published by Jonny McNee
May 2012
Second Printing June 2012
Third Printing August 2013
Copyright © 2012 by Jonny McNee

ISBN 978-0-9572157-0-2

jonnymcnee@googlemail.com

Printed in Northern Ireland.

CONTENTS

ACKNOWLEDGEMENTS

Many people and organisations gave freely of their time, expertise and patience to ensure that the Donegal Spitfire story could be told. The project owes its origins to a BBC NI series 'Dig WW2' filmed by Derry based 360 Production and I am extremely grateful to the series producer John Hayes Fisher and all the team at their Derry office for their support and for letting me participate in the series. Thanks are also due to my fellow diggers – Steve, Vickie, Gareth, Jeff, Glyn, Simon, Ian, Philippa, Baz and presenter Dan for all their assistance and fun times during the summer digs.

To the Wolfe empire – Betty, Barbara and Theo and the extended family, you trusted me when, as a complete stranger on the other side of the Atlantic, I approached you for your support and blessing for the dig. We have come a long way over the last 12 months! I am eternally grateful to Martin and Danny Kearney from Moneydarragh, Co Donegal. Without their help P8074 would still be lying beneath the peat.

I am truly indebted to Galen Weston and his team for the invite to Toronto and his support for the project. Thanks are also due to Lord Shaftesbury for letting us dig on his land. My sincere thanks to the Mayor of Derry Alderman Maurice Devenney for making Betty and Barbara feel so welcome and to the Derry City Council Heritage and Museum Service staff for all their support and assistance with the project and this book. Jacinta and Damien, thank you both for taking photographs throughout the project and thank you Tim for getting the text and photos ready for the printers. Martin, my sincere appreciation for all the metal display stands you designed and built for the exhibition.

In arranging the dig I had the pleasure of working with many organisations who decided this unique project deserved a chance to take flight. My thanks and appreciation to:

- Dave Hendee at the Omaha World Herald, Nebraska USA;
- Queens University Belfast – School of Geography, Archaeology and Palaeoecology;

- The Geological Survey of Northern Ireland;
- Archaeologists – Farrimond Macmanus Ltd;
- Northern Ireland Office – Protective Security Unit;
- PSNI – Firearms & Explosive Branch;
- Irish Defence Forces – Ordnance Company, 4 Logistics Support Battalion, Custume Barracks, Athlone;
- R Robinson & Son Quarry (Claudy);
- City of Derry Airport Management;
- Department of Environment, Heritage & Local Government (Republic of Ireland);
- National Museum Service of Ireland
- MOD – Joint Casualty and Compassionate Centre;
- Irish Defence Forces Military Archives, Dublin;
- Gardai (Moville);
- Department of the Environment – NIEA – Protecting Historic Monuments.

To my Mum, Dad, sister and brother, thank you for all your proof reading and support along the way. Finally to my wife Andree and children Dylan and Grace. My unending gratitude for your patience with P8074 over the last year and the late nights that were needed to make this book a reality. I couldn't have done it without you.

For Pilot Officer Roland 'Bud' Wolfe (1918 – 1994)
133 (Eagle) Squadron RAF

FOREWORD

The Story of the Donegal Spitfire describes an endeavor to literally dig up the past. This 21st Century enterprise bears certain resemblances to one our father, Roland "Bud" Wolfe, undertook over 70 years ago. Prior to US engagement in WWII, he joined the RAF to fly top-line combat fighters such as the Supermarine Spitfire. Each disparate commitment required equal measures of courage, foolhardiness, imagination, skill, intelligence, good fortune, stubborn perseverance, and, most importantly, faithful colleagues and families.

Jonny McNee's invitation to lend our names and good will to this WWII archaeological project produced a unique mix of trepidation and cautious amazement. As news spread among the "Wolfe Empire", and we considered a trip abroad, Cousin Jim affirmed, "This is history being made: We're there!" And so we were. To our delight, the past came back not to haunt us but to enrich our sense of Dad's early career. We find our personal histories given a new horizon. From the Curragh in County Kildare and Gleneely's boggy hills in County Donegal to the museums, mayoral chambers, and airport of Derry-Londonderry, we received warm greetings, kind attention and exquisite lessons in honoring the past.

We hold in high regard every individual contribution to this project. Many wonderful people gave untold hours of energy, compassion, love and plain hard work. From the lore and land of Donegal, they returned Spitfire P8074 to the light of day attended, as is any significant artefact, by the facts and the speculations that construct History from Story. As you read **The Story of the Donegal Spitfire**, we hope you experience the excitement, amazement and inspiration of its accomplishment.

In gratitude for families of birth, circumstance and generous spirit,

Betty Wolfe and Barbara Kurcharczyk.

USA

INTRODUCTION

Most people, even those with little aviation knowledge or interest, when asked to name an aircraft, would probably include the Supermarine Spitfire. World War 2 (WW2), and in particular the Battle of Britain, boosted its reputation to almost mythical proportions, the mixture of fact and fiction which enhanced its stature having been the source of constant debate ever since. Production started in 1937 and when it finally ended in 1949, a total of more than twenty-two thousand Spitfires had been built.

This book charts the story behind the discovery and excavation in June 2011 of just one of these iconic aircraft, a Mk IIa Spitfire serial number P8074 from 133 (Eagle) Squadron RAF. During WW2, this squadron was based for a few months at RAF Eglinton, some 7 miles north east of Derry, Northern Ireland. The story became known in the media as 'The Donegal Spitfire' and was the first licenced excavation of a WW2 aircraft anywhere on the island of Ireland. The book also covers the fascinating career of its American pilot, Pilot Officer Roland 'Bud' Wolfe who abandoned his stricken aircraft in November 1941 which then nosedived and buried itself deep beneath the peat on the Glenshinny mountain, in the townland of Moneydarragh, near Gleneely village on the Inishowen peninsula, Co Donegal.

It explains how I organised the project in the days after finding pieces of corroded airframe in a remote gully on the mountain in January 2011. It recollects the joyous highs and stressful lows in obtaining the required archaeological licences and permissions for a project that had never been attempted before. It records the nail biting tension of watching very expensive 24 ton diggers inching their way slowly across a waterlogged bog to take up their positions ready to attempt the recovery.

The story grew from the young volunteer American pilot parachuting to safety from his aircraft over Donegal to become headline news 70 years later in Ireland, America and Canada. The tale of his internment in neutral Eire, followed by a short-lived escape back to his squadron at RAF Eglinton and his subsequent re–internment under the orders of the RAF immediately grabbed the public imagination. The iconic fighter's war time donation by successful Canadian businessman Garfield Weston, its incredible state of preservation and the firing of one of its recovered Browning machine guns – watched by over a million people on the BBC website – catapulted the P8074 story onto a global stage.

'The Story of the Donegal Spitfire' culminates in the emotional visit to Derry by the pilot's two daughters and other members of the extended family to commemorate their father's war time career and launch the museum exhibition of recovered items. The discovery and excavation of Spitfire P8074 was recorded as part of a BBC NI series entitled 'Dig WW2' presented by Dan Snow and filmed by Derry based 360 Production. The series was broadcast in spring 2012.

CHAPTER 1

The Origins of Plan B

Poor old Spitfire P8074. To say it was a potential Plan B would be untrue. It wasn't even on a shortlist. No, P8074 was the last minute accident that spectacularly turned fate on its head; left coincidence in tatters and then took off and how!

Plan A was to find a Mk Vb Spitfire serial number BM557 from 152 Squadron that crashed on the former RAF war time airfield at Eglinton in May 1942. The airfield is now the site of the City of Derry Airport. The excavation of BM557 was to be filmed as part of a major BBC Northern Ireland co production with History Canada called Dig World War 2 (WW2) filmed by Derry television production company 360 Production. The aim of the series was to explore how military archaeology is uncovering the secrets of WW2. The series was to comprise of 3 episodes, each an hour long with an aircraft excavation to feature in each episode, as a 5 or 6 minute segment. The other two aviation digs had already been planned for England and France. As the series was being co produced by BBC NI, all involved were keen to have a Northern Ireland related aircraft excavation to feature in the series.

I had been searching for BM557 for nearly 20 years. The odds looked reasonably good. I had numerous eyewitnesses; now in their late 80's, but unfortunately they couldn't agree on the same location. Each of their indicated crash sites lay in different grassed areas which lay dotted between the runways in front of the airport terminal. I had several historical RAF documents detailing the crash and indicating an approximate area for the crash site, but this description in no way bore any resemblance to what these elderly gentlemen were telling me. I had a good quality aerial photograph of the airfield taken a few weeks after the crash. The Photographic Unit at the RAF Museum in Hendon, London studied it and with their experience, they pointed out one particular area that seemed to indicate evidence of a recently filled in crash crater. But frustratingly, its location didn't correlate with any of the descriptions contained in the historical RAF paperwork.

Also involved in the Dig WW2 series were an experienced team of aviation archaeologists from England and Wales. Between them they had a wealth of experience of finding and excavating WW2 aircraft since the early 1970's. With their specialist equipment and my local aviation knowledge, we genuinely thought this would be a straightforward search and recovery mission. All we had to do was walk up and down an area the size of 2 football pitches carrying a magnetometer until it beeped to indicate it had detected a deeply buried engine which weighed nearly three quarters of a ton. It wasn't really rocket science.

The searching at the airport began in earnest towards the end of 2010. By January 2011, we had searched every grassed area in front of the airport terminal. We searched in the wind, rain, snow and, on one occasion, the sun. Time after time the security personnel signed us in and wished us good luck and escorted the team around the runways. Time after time we dug up coins, old horseshoes and tin cans. Patiently the Air Traffic Control Manager would wish us better luck for the next time. At each of these searches, the cameras rolled. So I guess did the series producer's eyes.

After every fruitless search, I sat down again with all the evidence, talked to the eyewitnesses again to clarify their recollections and scrutinised the available war time photos. I rang organisations that used hi-tech ground penetrating radar equipment to enquire if they could assist with the search. As soon as I mentioned the Spitfire word, I found people were very keen to help. I had many conversations with professional people who admitted to gluing themselves to the kitchen table during their Airfix years. The Geological Survey of Northern Ireland and Queens University Belfast (QUB) joined forces and spent a day walking up and down with the most advanced search equipment available in Northern Ireland, but still... nothing! Although they did detect a 'V' shaped profile beneath the grass in one area, very representative of a filled in high speed impact crater, their equipment detected no metal associated with this feature. All we did find were several war time flare cartridge cases. Silently and frustratingly in the background on all these search days, the cameras continued to roll, recording us endlessly searching but never finding. With the clock ticking and nothing to show yet for our efforts Dig WW2 was possibly not going to contain a Northern Ireland related aviation dig.

It came to pass, in early January 2011 as we walked away from yet another fruitless search at the airport that the producer of the series John Hayes Fisher (by now a slightly troubled man) walked up beside me and said:

"You know filming you lot walking up and down and finding nothing is not terribly exciting, the series is called Dig WW2 after all!"

I could understand his frustrations. 360 Production were footing the bill for each of these unproductive days and had a tight filming deadline to meet. In addition, my search for this elusive aircraft was rapidly becoming the focus of good natured banter from my family, friends and work colleagues.

"Do you know of any other aircraft from here that crashed?" John added desperately.

Desperately I stood thinking for a few minutes. I announced I knew of a Spitfire crash in Donegal. However this Spitfire was so lost in a large expanse of featureless mountain moor that no-one had ever found it. Undeterred by his silence to this announcement, I offered to go looking to find this aircraft.

Unenthusiastic expressions of 'Good luck with that one' emanated from the rest of the team and our frustrated producer as we trudged towards the terminal.

Home I went and asked my daughter Grace did she want to go plane hunting one weekend.

"Will we find it Daddy?" she asked innocently.

"Not a chance" I replied honestly, "but Daddy promised a man he would search a mountain to find it."

The next couple of weeks were spent assembling what little written evidence existed about this crash. Most books or web sites about war time crashes in Ireland all stated the same basic information:

30th November 1941 - Spitfire P8074 - 133 Squadron. Crashed 3.5 miles North at Glenshinny, in the townland of Moneydarragh, Co Donegal.

Other anecdotal evidence suggested an attempted partial recovery in the days after the crash by the Irish Army. Documents from the time suggested only a couple of machine guns and some surface fragments were recovered. Either way, it soon became apparent that no one had a detailed map with a helpful 'X' marked on it.

Slowly but surely, I accumulated further information about what had happened to this aircraft. The pilot's engine had overheated; it crashed into a bog; the majority of the aircraft was still apparently buried at the site and the pilot was called Roland 'Bud' Wolfe from Nebraska. What a coincidence I thought. My own brother lived and worked in Nebraska. Little did I realise then, that as coincidences go, this one would be very minor in the scale of things to come.

As my priority was to find the actual location of the crash site, I must admit at the time I rather overlooked another little fact I found:

…the pilot was interned in the Curragh, almost immediately broke parole, went north, was handed back and eventually was released in 1943.

My blinkered attitude ensured that this aspect of the story was filed away in my head under 'Miscellaneous'. My focus was narrow – find the plane first.

I was also aware that if I ever did discover this Spitfire, the search and everything after was likely to be filmed for the BBC NI series. Therefore it was essential that all aspects of any potential dig were done correctly and legally. This brings us to the legislation part and it was here that things really started to get complicated.

This Spitfire, wherever it lay buried in Co Donegal, remained, according to the UK legislation, the property of the Crown under the Protection of Military Remains Act 1986. This Act applies to the UK and it is the MOD Commemorations & Licensing Centre at Imjin Barracks in Gloucester that considers all requests to excavate such aircraft through the granting of a licence under the Act. First potential hiccup I thought. Clearly the UK

Act cannot apply to Co Donegal in the Republic of Ireland, so how will it legislate for what I want to do?

My email explaining this predicament was the beginning of an excellent working relationship with the two ladies responsible for this centre. They acknowledged my excavation proposal in Co Donegal was unique, and likely to be fraught with transboundary legislative issues. They explained that although the Act didn't apply to Co Donegal, the remains of the aircraft still remained the property of the Crown. However they stated they would work with me to make it happen as best they could. I felt rather reassured that I had the support of the MOD on my side.

Next stop was to establish contact with the relevant people in the Department of the Environment, Heritage & Local Government (DEHLG) in Dublin who are the responsible authority for administering the archaeological legislation in the Republic of Ireland. I was seeking quick answers to fundamental questions;
• Did they consider a crashed 70 year old Spitfire to be an archaeological object under their legislation?;
• If 'yes', what licences were required?;
• Had they licenced such a proposal before?; and finally
• Would they let me do it?

The rather stunned lady from DEHLG who took my details promised to get back to me. With that phone call I probably became, over the next few months, the biggest pain in the ass to those archaeological officials in Dublin, who probably preferred their archaeology to be polished, made of flint and 6000 years old. At around the same time, I contacted the Military Archives at Cathal Brugha Barracks in Dublin. There, amongst many wonderful collections of historic military documents, they retained all the original WW2 files pertaining to the Intelligence Section (known as G2) of the Irish Army. It was this section that would have investigated and written up the details of the crash as soon as it had occurred.

The staff at the Archive were a tremendous help. Sensing that my project was big in scale and short on time, they side stepped the usual Archive arrangements that would have required me to book an appointment and travel to Dublin to search through countless boxes. Quickly, they scanned several letters from a copy file that existed on the crash and emailed them to me. In an instant I was transported back to 1941. Here were letters detailing the events of the crash, the officers who investigated it and more importantly confirming that only a few items were retrieved at the time of the crash. The letters stated that the significant majority of the aircraft was left deeply buried in the peat. No map – but it was a start! The Archive staff also sent me a picture of Pilot Officer Roland 'Bud' Wolfe with his RAF hat perched jauntily on his head.

As promised, the DEHLG officials quickly got back to me to gather more facts and put me in touch with the archaeologist who covered the Donegal region. Up to this point, I suspect he had probably been enjoying a pleasant existence administering to the requirements of traditional archaeology. Now he was effectively been asked to consider the excavation of a plane crash that only happened 70 years ago. There was no precedent for this in Ireland. Nothing he could turn to for reference.

I also sent an email to the Editor of the Omaha World Herald in Omaha, Nebraska, USA asking would the paper be prepared to run a story to assist me in tracing either the pilot, if he was still alive, or his relatives.

At this stage, it appears my time was more or less spent starting ripples. Emails were lobbed in all directions. Some disappeared without trace, most came back bringing a small sprig of information, but a few, out of sight, were gathering speed and form around the globe to eventually return as tidal waves.

These were hectic times and late nights on the home computer. My patient wife slowly realised she was losing me to 'my other woman in Donegal'. I don't recall thinking at that time I was being overwhelmed by what I had started or daunted in my task. I was not alone in what was becoming my epic quest. I was gathering around me the aviation equivalent of the Knights Templar. Our noble crusade was underway. Well almost. First I had to find out how to get to Moneydarragh.

CHAPTER 2

Fate and Chocolate Buttons

The 30th of January 2011 was a Sunday. Just another bitterly cold day in amongst the many we had at that time. As I watched the wind trying to prise the frozen leaves off the ground, I honestly thought that what I was about to do was a complete waste of my time and expensive diesel.

I was 100% certain that I had no hope at all of driving out into the middle of the Inishowen Peninsula in Co Donegal and stumbling over the crash site. Not a chance. Mountain crashes like this I knew took months, even years, of walking up and down before finding anything of interest. Anyway, I consoled myself; we'll find BM577 at the airport soon, so we won't need this Spitfire anyway.

To be truthful, the only reason my daughter Grace and I went out that day was because I had promised producer John and the team that I would go looking. So out we went to the vast upland bog within the townland of Moneydarragh, where according to the not very helpful RAF records: *a Spitfire crashed 3.5 miles North of Glenshinny*. Glenshinny is a windswept, boggy mountain in the townland of Moneydarragh, which is some 7miles north west of Moville on the Inishowen Peninsula, Co Donegal.

Although I was optimistically downbeat about our chances, hunting for these sites still generates a bit of excitement. Grace and I joked about how we were going to fit the aircraft into our car boot for the journey back. We joked all the way to Moville but the laughing stopped as we approached the village of Gleneely. To our left, under the low clouds that spat squalls of rain, brooded Glenshinny mountain. A ripple of despair and frustration took hold of me. Did I really want to be walking up and down a mountain with 6 year old Grace who had a fondness for falling into puddles?

"I'm hungry" she announced from the back seat. "I want chocolate – chocolate helps you find planes!"

A small petrol station came into view as we approached the village of Gleneely. McLaughlin's Store was quiet as we parked in the forecourt. We got out and looked back up at the taunting mass of Glenshinny mountain.

Inside the shop, Grace picked up a packet of chocolate buttons and we went up to the till. The lady behind the counter asked Grace what brought her out to Gleneely on such a cold day.

"We are looking for Spitfires" she replied matter of factly.

Now to be fair, any other shop assistant would have said "That's nice dear" and handed Grace her change, but this lady, Katie McLaughlin, to her eternal credit was interested in local history and the conversation, without any embellishment at all, progressed as follows:

"Spitfires?" she replied "I don't know anything about Spitfires, but I know of a plane that crashed near here during the war"

My heart soared, could she know something?

"Round near Glengad head" she continued. At that point, I knew she was talking about a different aircraft, a much larger Liberator bomber.

I politely replied that sadly that crash was not the one we were looking for today.

She was interested to know that there was a local crash near to her village and apologised that she could be of no further help. As we turned to leave she added:

"The person you need to talk to is Kieran Faulkner, he might know of this crash, but I haven't seen him in months".

Grace and I thanked her for her help and as we walked towards the shop door, we paused to let a man in.

"Kieran!" exclaimed the shop assistant "that's Kieran!" "That's the man I was just talking about".

It was true. Kieran Faulkner, the man she hadn't seen in months and who just might know something about this crash, had by complete chance walked into the same shop in Gleneely. After a few seconds of staring at each other, I explained the twist of fate in bumping into him and the details behind our needle in a haystack search.

"Oh aye, the Spitfire crash, American guy....it's up in the mountains somewhere..don't know where…"

My emotions were on a rollercoaster, for a few minutes as he talked knowingly about not knowing where it was. He apologised again for knowing little else, but he said the person who would know was called Martin Kearney.

"But.." said Kieran.

I sensed crushing news was coming.

"I haven't seen him in ages".

I grinned politely through gritted teeth and turned to usher Grace through the door. I think it was the way Katie squeaked "Martin Kearney", that made me turn and look at her to see was she OK.

She was pointing out the window at a man who was getting out of his car.

"That's Martin Kearney!!" she said slowly.

Grace poked me in the ribs and said "Oh Daddy, this is so spooky!"

Beckoned into the store by Katie waving frantically at him through the shop window, Martin Kearney entered the shop to be confronted by 4 open mouthed people, all commonly afflicted, to varying degrees, with speechlessness.

The staring, pointing and assorted saint praising seemed to last a lifetime. Trying to summon up a manly voice befitting our noble quest, I said I had come to Gleneely in search of a Spitfire.

"Oh yes, the American one, from Eglinton..what about it?" questioned Martin.

"Do you know roughly where it is; could you point out an area on a map?" I stuttered.

"I have to go to Carndonagh now, come to my house at 1pm and I'll take you to the crash site. I've been many times, there are still wee bits of it lying scattered around under the rushes." "That wee one" he smiled pointing at Grace "will get them among the rushes" I memorised the directions he gave me to get to his house, wrote down his phone number and with that Martin paid for his fuel and drove off to the nearby town of Carndonagh.

Bewildered the 4 of us stood looking at each. "Did that just happen?" I asked the assistant. We all knew something genuinely special had just happened in McLaughlin's store.

"Good luck with the search", said Kieran shaking my hand. "How long were you looking for this plane?"

I looked at my watch. "6 minutes" I replied. It was true. From the minute we arrived at that store, 6 short fateful minutes had passed. Now I was walking out the door with the name of a man who, in one hour's time, was going to take me straight to the crash site. Katie gave us a cheery wave as we left "I think this plane wants you two to find it" she laughed.

Gibbering with excitement, Grace and I spent the next hour walking across a nearby windswept beach with big grins on our faces. The time quickly passed and soon it was time to go and meet Martin.

A slight panic set in on the way back as I realised that I was having difficulty remembering Martin's directions. I hadn't written them down. Great! – the one guy who knows where this plane is and I mess up his directions to his house.

I pulled in beside a house and tried to ring his number. Marvellous! – no signal on my phone! I turned to tell Grace in the back seat that Daddy might be lost and was startled to see Martin's face peering in the passenger window. By chance, in the middle of nowhere, I had parked outside his house. He took us through a twisting maze of roads, lanes and tracks until we stopped. We emptied out of the car into a biting wind and looked up a rising expanse of desolate moorland slashed with incised streams.

"See that deep gully there?" Martin pointed off into the distance, "Your plane is up near the top of that" He recalled that his father had visited the site the day after the crash and often told Martin the story of the crash and his memories of the site in the days and weeks after. Over the years, people cutting peat had stripped the site of any visible bits, and now only one or two people had a rough idea of the crash location.

Another squall sent us dashing into the car. As we drove back to Martin's house, he said he would be keen to help and find out more about this local crash. He said a friend of his also knew of the possible crash location and he would speak to him during the week. We arranged to meet up again the next free weekend I had. We swopped details and I thanked him again profusely for his assistance. We all agreed fate had been good to us this day.

Grace and I drove home shell-shocked. When we got home, we casually announced that we had gone to Gleneely, found the crash site and all was well with the world. I remember that this was greeted with a fair degree of scepticism at first. No, we didn't actually get to see a lovely crash crater and no, we didn't get to see any bits of aluminium, but we had narrowed down the entire mountain to one steep gully area. That was finding it as far as Grace and I were concerned. In two weeks time, we were going back to that gully with Martin and his friend. We were going to find that plane!

In the days immediately after, I felt like the child walking into the living room on Boxing Day, knowing that despite a room full of toys, some of the excitement had gone and Christmas was another year away. The thrill of the hunt, albeit a very quick hunt and the expectation that went with it was now over. I realised that I was now faced with a potentially uphill bureaucratic struggle to obtain the necessary licences to progress the project. This was the hard part. This was to be my lone battle.

When I rang the authorities to tell them I had found the crash site, I thought I could detect surprise at the other end of the phone. The officials probably hadn't expected me to find the crash site. So you can imagine I thought they didn't mirror my excitement, when, having told them I had found the crash site, I asked for a copy of the application form to request a Detection Licence.

This is a simple little form. It requests information on the location, landowner's details and the equipment to be used. This immediately required me to establish who the land owner was and seek his or her permission. The locals considered it was Lord Shaftesbury. Just my luck! It couldn't be a local farmer who I could go and visit. No - it had to be Lord Shaftesbury, who lives in Dorset, England. So I opened another file and began discussions with his Estate Manager.

During conversations at this time, the officials at the DEHLG suggested that they understood the site had been extensively dug over and substantial remains removed. This was a bit of a bombshell. I didn't know whether this was based on written historical evidence they had access to or possibly they were confusing it with the war time salvage attempt in 1941. I quickly contacted the Military Archive services and Martin in Moneydarragh in an attempt to shed some light on this claim. There was nothing in the files apart from a reference to limited salvage at the time of the crash. Martin could not recall his father mentioning any other war time salvage attempts or any others in later years.

Almost daily, the complexity of what I was undertaking became more twisted and convoluted and I could see a brick wall looming. In a nutshell, it appeared that the core of the issue was that the DEHLG naturally considered that, under their National Monuments Act, the remains belonged to them because they lay in Co Donegal. Furthermore, they considered the remains as an archaeological object and as such it was subject to a plethora of licencing legislation. On the other hand, the MOD were very adamant that the ownership of the aircraft belonged to the Crown. This had battle written all over it.

While I steered a sensitive and diplomatic course between all the parties, I also had to establish land ownership with Lord Shaftesbury. His Estate Manager, Philip Rymer, was very interested in the project and was excellent in this liaison role. He quickly established that they did in fact own this land. They had to go looking through a very impressive leather bound book, dating from 1863 to establish this. He was very understanding that at this stage, we were just looking for permission to legally access their land with surveying equipment. It could transpire that we might find nothing and the project would end at this stage. But he was optimistic and wished us well. He hoped we would find it and if we did have to dig a small hole in his moor at a later stage then that also looked possible.

So the landowner appeared happy, but could I persuade the authorities to grant me a detection licence? It was very frustrating. I couldn't find the Spitfire at the airport which in theory should have been the easy one, but I could find the difficult one, then only to fear that I may not be able to dig it up. My blood pressure was not good at this stage.

Looking back this was probably the most intense period of sensitive negotiation during the entire project. The licencing authorities politely jockeyed for position over who owned the remains and in addition I assumed that DEHLG officials were hopefully praying that I couldn't pin point the exact crash site. All the time, the remainder of the Dig WW2 filming schedule was ongoing and the rest of the aviation team were becoming frustrated at the ongoing licencing fuss and the lack of progress.

In England, Scotland and Wales, it is relatively straightforward. The recovery of WW2 aviation aircraft remains is administered by the MOD under the Protection of Military Remains Act (PMRA) 1986, but there isn't the same parallel legislation requirement for the remains to be treated and licenced as an archaeological object. Some local Councils in these jurisdictions may ask you to provide some form of archaeological methodology but it doesn't appear to be a widely held requirement.

However in NI, there is an additional requirement to be compliant with the Historic Monuments and Archaeological Objects (Northern Ireland) Order 1995. This local archaeological legislation works in conjunction with the UK wide MOD Act, and considers that any buried aircraft is an archaeological object. It requires a licence to be granted under its provision as well as the MOD licence under the PMRA.

The relevant authorities in the Republic of Ireland follow a similar approach to NI. It was this additional hierarchy of licencing and consideration of crashed planes as archaeological objects that frustrated the rest of the aviation team. They didn't have this issue in England or Wales, but eventually they came round to the fact that the plane was in the Republic of Ireland and their rules applied.

To be honest, for all my grumbling, I have to respect this approach that the authorities both North and South have adopted. Doing it this way, a licencing requirement at each stage, meant I and the authorities knew exactly what I was undertaking at each stage. It was a map by which I could hopefully progress towards an excavation. Unfortunately what I was asking to do was a first. Worryingly, it appeared that non-archaeologically qualified sorts like me weren't granted Licences to Detect. I applied anyway and the officials in Dublin retired to consider how to progress my application.

The 14th of February was a fair day on the mountain. The sun tried to smile a few rays in our direction. Just after noon, Martin and his friend Tommy Lafferty pulled up beside us in the lay-by. This time, we were heading to the gully from the opposite direction from where we had first viewed it in January. We squelched our way across the moor and on to a flat descending plain that eventually swept down to a steep slope punctuated with streams flowing in deep hidden channels. Just beneath the crest of this slope, Tommy pointed at a brown bank of peat with a stream flowing from the base of it.

"There" he said casually pointing at the small, rushy depression that surrounded the stream. "That's where the plane went in". There was no fanfare, no great build up or wild back slapping. It was very matter of fact. There it was, underneath our feet somewhere. Grace headed off and soon was scampering around under the rushes like a demented spaniel. Suddenly she stood up in the midst of a thick clump "Is this it?" She was waving a bit of metal, a bit of corroded aircraft aluminium. Soon she had flushed a few other pieces from deep in the rushes. A brief look in the stream uncovered several other pieces. A Spitfire had crashed on this mountain. I was standing in a gentle depression, holding pieces of corroded aluminium. Could I dare to make the presumption that this was it?

If it was it, I thought as we walked back off the mountain, what was I supposed to do next with it? A myriad of thoughts bounced around excitedly inside my head. Permissions, logistics, expenses – all those annoying little trivial matters! I strode proudly off the mountain, drove home and rang producer John.

"John – you know that impossible Spitfire in Donegal?"

"Yes…"

"I found it!"

"Fantastic Jonny - where is it?" he gushed.

"It's up a mountain, in the middle of a bog, in a steep gully" I explained.

There was a long silence.

Then on 16th February, at 9 33 am, an email announced that Detection Licence number 11R0018 had been approved and I was licenced to legally detect over the crash site. It was time to assemble the team from all over the UK. It was game on!

CHAPTER 3

Our Finest Hour

The 25th of February 2011 found me sitting at Belfast International Airport at some ungodly hour in the morning to collect an assorted bunch of characters, who collectively, are probably the UK's premier aviation recovery team. Gareth Jones, Glyn Morgan and Jeff Carless fell off the early morning flight from Luton. The other team stalwart Steve Vizard was unavailable for this search date. After several large airport coffees to bring them round to a state which at least encouraged conversation, we slowly slithered our way back to Derry. Northern Ireland at that stage was experiencing one of those rare defrosting days in between the long ice age that had descended on the land.

Just before noon, having collected photographer friend Damien Gallagher, who had offered to brave the elements and capture the day's events, we drove into the car park of a local hotel, just outside Moville. Here we met up with the rest of the 360 Production film team. The plan was to film the search at the Moneydarragh site and then next day do the same at the City of Derry Airport for Spitfire BM557. Effectively this was the last throw of the dice for a Northern Ireland related WW2 air crash to potentially feature in Dig WW2. My feelings were mixed and confused. On one hand, I had a crash site in a deep bog in the middle of Donegal in a sloping incised gully. On the other I had a Spitfire buried somewhere in a small grassed flat area in front of the terminal at the airport. I had 3 living eyewitnesses, all the documents and photographs you could want. I had also secured a licence to search for and, if we found it, excavate this aircraft from the archaeologists at the Protecting Historic Monument Unit, Northern Ireland Environment Agency (NIEA), Department of the Environment. The only fly in the ointment was that at the possibly undiggable Donegal site I had found scattered fragments after 5 minutes of looking. At the airport site I had nothing to show for nearly 20 years of searching.

We assembled at the roadside next to the bleak desolate moor. It appeared as cold and uninviting as the day Bud Wolfe baled out over it 70 years ago.

Mustering as much enthusiasm as I could, I pointed out to producer John the proposed landscape; the ankle wrenching bogs and the deep, heather hidden gullies. As a warning to others, never point these or similar features out to anyone you want to motivate, you'll only end up depressing them. The aviation searchers, the production team, the camera and sound team kitted up and set out across the heather to meet Martin Kearney and his friend Tommy who I had arranged to join us at the potential crash site.

John explained to us the shots he wanted. I quickly learnt that to shoot a short sequence of someone just saying 'Hello' to someone else requires these people to be filmed up close; near and even faraway. There were 'noddy head' shots and expression shots. It takes forever to film a 30 second on-screen 'Hello'. John will probably call me a philistine (or possibly worse!) for criticizing his art, but I was a complete novice television person who was keen to get on with finding this iconic WW2 fighter – I was chomping at the bit. Eventually after filming the moor from a multitude of angles, we were let loose with our equipment to begin searching this steep gully. We were using a mix of metal detectors and magnetometers. The metal detectors were ideal for pinpointing scattered fragments located on or just under the surface. The more powerful magnetometers could detect as far down as 35ft and were used to detect the presence of substantial remains, such as the engine, undercarriage or weapons. I proudly led the team to the area in the gully were I had earlier in the month found the scattered fragments of corroded aluminium. 'Definitely aircraft' was the considered opinion, when we immediately located more weathered pieces. This was going to be a piece of cake I thought. We could possibly be back in the pub within the hour, defrosting and celebrating.

Gareth, Jeff, Glyn and I divided the immediate area into search areas and off we went searching. Every now and then, John would put a camera on us and ask what we had found. 'More fragments…plenty of corroded fragments…surface bits'. These phrases soon became frequently repeated lines to take when a camera appeared at the end of your nose. Other things that appeared on our noses were colossal drips. It was freezing. Frequently, just before filming would start, Emma our production assistant would shout 'Boys..noses!' and we would reach for whatever was handy to make our noses respectable.

With no eureka moment forthcoming, slowly over a couple of hours, the enthusiastic mood of the team began to wane. The cigarette breaks began to take longer, the looks became more despairing and the smiles more forced. John and the film team retreated upslope and sat in the heather watching as we scrambled up and down the moor finding plenty of old corroded surface bits and nothing else. Late in the afternoon, I walked down to the end of the gully by myself and sat down at the base of a stunted mountain ash tree and talked to a sheep that was huddled down in the ravine, taking shelter from the wind. It had the most relaxed look on its face as it chewed away on a mouthful of grass. I remember telling the sheep my problems and how unfair it was that Bud had crashed this plane obviously somewhere nearby but yet we couldn't pin point the exact crash site. As the light began to fade, I bid the sheep farewell and looking at the sky, I asked Bud if there was any chance of help.

The team regrouped, but by now the enthusiasm was almost gone. All we had to show were sore legs, red noses and the beginnings of mild hypothermia. Even the hardy mountain men, Martin and Tommy had long since retreated to the warmth of their homes. The highlight of their day had been me standing on a Red Grouse. Tommy said it was the first one he had seen on the moor in probably 20 years.

During one of numerous regroupings, Gareth and I discussed the locations where we were finding these fragments and tried to rationalise their significance. Martin had told us earlier in the day that a significant portion of wing had been dragged down slope and now lay entwined in a hedge further down the gully. He added people coming from Gleneely during and after the war years would have come from down-slope, and walked up the gully to see the crash site, or more likely, to cut and gather peat. Gareth and I surmised the fragments we were finding were 70 year old bits that had lain on the surface since the time of the crash. They had been exposed to the elements and had either been washed down slope over the years or left behind, as discarded souvenirs by the villagers as they walked back down to the village. So we searched higher above the gully and found nothing! This was the final nail in the coffin for me. I was resigned to the fact my spitfire finding efforts for this series were over. Frustratingly I couldn't find this one despite the clear presence of aircraft aluminium in the vicinity. Tomorrow at the airport I knew, despite all our bravado and optimism, was going to be yet another frustrating waste of a day.

John assembled the troops and tried to rally us for tomorrow. It was time to call it a day in the fading light. It was time to go back to the hotel in Derry and defrost, get a good dinner and discuss strategy for tomorrow. With a very heavy heart, we admitted defeat. The camera and sound team began to dismantle their kit and carefully pick their way across the moor in the encroaching evening. Anyone watching this sorry spectacle would have seen a sad procession of individuals, stretched across the mountainside and united in silence. The 360 team crossed the skyline and were soon out of view. Bringing up the rear was Jeff and myself. I had a spade and a metal detector. Jeff was armed with a magnetometer. That morning as we headed from our cars down to the possible crash site, we had followed a little sheep path that ran along the edge of a steep slope. As we staggered, exhausted and depressed, on our way back, Jeff and I walked about 20 − 30 ft out from this path, actually in the moor itself. We puffed and panted our way out of the gully, up a steep slope and crested a rise onto a more level area of bog that stretched out to the road and the relative shelter of our cars.

And as we lurched over this rise, Jeff stumbled and threw out his magnetometer to support himself. Now, normally after such a frustrating day, at this point I should have laughed out loud at Jeff's misfortune. However as he fell forward onto the ground, something happened that made me instantaneously put aside thoughts of laughter and smart one-liners. The ground rippled. Nothing obvious − but just enough to show that this immediate area was not like the other surrounding moor surface. I went to Jeff's assistance. It was immediately clear that he too was thinking along similar lines. "Are you thinking what I'm thinking?" was the first thing he said to me. Like two kids with a new trampoline for Christmas, we began to bounce up and down on the surface. As we looked around we saw we were standing in a very subtle oval shaped depression.

A few seconds later, we both noticed his magnetometer was emitting a low wail. The most heart warming noise you could ever wish to hear on a cold murky evening. "I think this is it, I think this is it!" Jeff kept repeating.

I roared at Gareth and Glyn to come back and join us at this spot. They in turn shouted at the 360 team to return. I recall John shouting from somewhere in the distance "What's up?" and someone replying "We got it, we got it – get your cameras out again!"

There is nothing to adequately describe that instantaneous rocket-like launch from depression to elation. In terms of euphoria, Jeff and I had just pulled 10G's.

Cold hands fumbled to re-assemble cameras, radio mikes were wired up again and unfortunately noses streamed yet again in torrents as we became increasingly excited. John called his lively cast to order and filmed the spontaneous mood as it unfolded. In a ballet like sequence we waltzed around our crater explaining the readings we were getting and interpreting what they could be.

"And here's our engine" we confidently announced before pirouetting to port and starboard to point out, with flourishing hand gestures, the possible location of the machine guns.

We sunk our probing rods deep into the crater and were rewarded with glorious metallic clunks. Hysterical uncontrollable laughter was not far from my lips. Our licence to detect technically did not permit us to undertake any excavation, but we felt that a small spade width hole was in order to ensure we were actually over the crash site and not at the grave of a long lost tractor. So in a rain soaked bog, we dug a small hole – 9 inches wide at most. It instantaneously filled with water. About a foot down the spade bounced off metal.

"Get down beside the hole Jonny!" instructed John, "I want this as it happens". So down I got onto the wet moor surface and crawled on my belly towards the small hole. Behind me, the rest of the team twisted and contorted themselves to get a good view of what was happening.

Hardly daring to breathe I pushed my hand down into the icy peaty sludge. John asked me to describe what I felt. At that precise moment in time, I felt two things. The first was the similarity to the following description of the moments immediately prior to the discovery of Tutankhamen's tomb.

He did not yet know at that point whether it was "a tomb or merely a cache", but he did see a promising sealed doorway between two sentinel statues. When Carnarvon asked "can you see anything?", Carter replied: "Yes, wonderful things."

The second was a very unpleasant tearing sensation, closely followed by pain, as my fingers were filleted by sharp jagged metal. I fished around and located a loose piece of metal and hoisted it triumphant into the fading evening light.

Gareth quickly wiped the piece down for it was covered in peat and blood. Emma apologised profusely for forgetting the first aid kit and for having no plasters. Gareth cheered, he had found a stamp number on this little piece of gleaming aircraft aluminium that bore the prefix '300' which is unique to Spitfires. The piece still carried its original camouflage paint scheme. "Definitely Spitfire!" he announced and it was handshakes all round.

John then asked for a quick piece to camera. I tried but failed dismally to look composed. John enquired could I stop waving my hands around as the blood was rather off putting. Emma said sorry again. We compromised that I could wave my remaining good hand as I excitedly explained what had just happened.

I recalled an email that Paul Logue, a Senior Inspector with the Historic Monuments Unit in the Department of the Environment sent me at 9 47am on the 15th September 2010. It was in response to our ongoing but fruitless search for the Spitfire at the City of Derry airport.
He said and I quote:

Welcome to our world Jonny. What usually happens is that you find what you're looking for in the last hour on the last afternoon of the last day. Hope your luck gets better.

The final irony came several days later when Damien, our photographer on the day, sent me a disc of all the photographs he had taken on the day. One of the very first ones was the group, descending into the deep gully with all our equipment. The camera crew brought up the rear. Where did Damien stand to take the picture? Slap in the middle of that very elusive crater where we later found the Spitfire!

The following Monday, my happy email explaining our joyous news rushed like an excited puppy down the wires to the National Monuments Unit of the Department of the Environment, Heritage & Local Government in Dublin where I imagine it was immediately told it was a bad dog and promptly banished to the garden. They probably also viewed my request for a Licence to Excavate with a sense of trepidation.

Meanwhile in my world, were the corks were still popping and a permanent grin was attached to my face, I sat down with a blank piece of paper and tried to map out what to do next. Having got this far, I was now more determined than ever to put every ounce of my energy into obtaining this licence. I knew what I was proposing was a first and would be a struggle. We had found the site; our initial survey indicated substantial remains were there, so why walk away now just because red tape potentially stood in the way?

However, regardless of my determination, I tempered my excitement with the reality of the crash site location. It was nearly half a kilometre away from a narrow, winding mountain road. It was deep peat with water filled trenches everywhere. The irony of getting an excavation licence, but finding the site was undiggable, was a distinct possibility.

The following days and weeks were a team effort as we advanced a plan. Gareth, Steve, Jeff and Glyn supplied a shopping list of equipment we would need to undertake such a precarious excavation. It was all very matter of fact. Apparently all I needed to rustle up were a couple of very large diggers, some bog mats and heavy duty water pumps. To their list, I considered adding the caveat that it may be beneficial if the digger owner and driver were certified clinically insane. Would anyone really want to drive a 25 ton digger out into the middle of this bog? Around this time I also began initial discussions with the Heritage and Museum Service staff at Derry

City Council to ascertain their thoughts on the project and would they be interested in displaying a Spitfire – should it surface!

360 Production had previously worked with the management of the National Museum in Dublin on a very successful Timewatch programme about Bog Bodies. Using these same contacts, they too liaised in order to assure the licencing authorities that our proposed project would be done by the book and in complete accordance with the relevant legislation. But first the licencing authorities wanted further proof that this indeed was the site and that substantial remains were buried at the site. It appeared they wanted irrefutable evidence before they would warrant the approval of such an excavation.

It was time to start pulling in the big guns. A very experienced team of GIS surveyors from Queens University Belfast had allowed themselves to be roped into previous searches for Spitfire BM557 at the City of Derry Airport. With many 'ologies and titles to their names, Alastair Ruffell, Jennifer McKinley and Conor Graham from the School of Geography, Archaeology and Palaeoecology felt that assisting me in the search for this buried aircraft represented a novel way of challenging their equipment, research models and field craft. They thought it would be a great day out to walk about in the middle of a deep bog and use their very expensive equipment in a manner for which it was not designed. They intended to use a very complicated Ground Penetrating Radar machine to bounce signals into the bog and demonstrate, by means of recording the signals that were bounced back from metallic items, the extent and depth of what lurked beneath.

While all this was going on, the day job still had to be done and the evenings were becoming tiring and monotonous. After the kids were put to bed, I jumped on the computer and typed to people about progress, equipment needs and answered requests from the licencing authorities into the wee small hours. I say monotonous, my wife had other names for it. Most of them unprintable and several of them physically impossible.

This period was probably the most intense time in the preparation. This was the spinning plate time. The Application to Excavate posed the sort of questions that quite rightly required a considered response. Although it was incredibly frustrating at the time to complete, it actually turned out to be time well spent because the preparation it required at this stage turned out to be extremely beneficial later. In fact it served as a route map for how the project would plan out on the day and in the subsequent days after excavation.

During this time I also had to initiate discussions with the Garda Siochana- the Irish Police in Moville, Co. Donegal and undertake research on the availability of specialist digger firms. There were early talks about potential excavation budgets with 360 Production and more discussions about our proposals with the landowner Lord Shaftesbury. My files soon expanded, the hours at the computer increased and slowly but surely this little snowball of a project began to gather momentum.

Sunday 13th March was the chosen date to meet on the moor with the QUB team. The weather was quite simply atrocious. It was bitterly cold and occasional stinging showers of hailstones peppered our faces. Reminiscent of early Antarctic explorers, we forced our way through the gale and out to the crash site, where we quickly subjected the crater to various ground penetrating radar surveys to ascertain what lay beneath. Using sign language to be understood above the roaring gale, I quickly learnt that the QUB team reckoned there was 'a lot' of Spitfire beneath the peat. They pointed to the video display on their radar machine to prove it. It clearly showed the presence of a large, metallic mass stretching from 6 meters down to a depth of about 10 meters. Delighted with these results, we packed up and struggled back through the gale towards the road. Dr Ruffell and I having agreed first, that if we didn't make it back to the cars, we would eat Conor, the GIS Research Officer first.

While all this was going on, I somehow found the time to complete a draft Application to Excavate Licence and work up a Method Statement as to how the project would unfold. I felt that a Method Statement, although not compulsory, was the best way of presenting this new area of archaeological research and excavation to the relevant authorities in Dublin. Hopefully this 60 page document with a supporting Appendix would contain all the information the archaeological authorities were seeking in response to the questions contained in a Licence to Excavate application form. There were details on the group composition and our previous experience, the finance side of things, how the dig would be undertaken, how the recovered items would be cleaned and where they would be displayed….plus 101 other key points to show that we had all bases covered.

We signed up a professional archaeologist called Ciara MacManus who was licenced to operate in both the North and the South. She would oversee the excavation on the day and ensure that it was undertaken professionally within archaeological parameters. Although as a team of 'aviation archaeologist's' we had many hundreds of licenced digs to our credit, we were still not considered as professional archaeologists by the Dublin authorities, so it was an essential part of our project application that we had a professional archaeologist on board.

Then in early March, while I was still drafting my Method Statement, the archaeological authorities responded to producer John and myself on several key issues that our proposed excavation posed. The Keeper of Irish Antiquities from the National Museum Service, Eamonn Kelly, in an exchange of emails with us, outlined a potential way forward. Eamonn and John had worked together on a previous archaeological television series and were well aware of each others reputations and professional approach. Eamonn outlined that my requests for the relevant licences was completely without precedent in their experience. As a result the Dublin authorities were naturally cautious as they were being asked to leave their archaeological comfort zone. Encouragingly he highlighted particular areas, such as the sections on preservation and display, which he advised I should complete in significant detail. He also suggested a range of other issues that he felt should be covered.

In addition, he outlined his role in the consultation process. The National Monuments Unit of the Department of Environment, Heritage and Local Government in Dublin, when determining my application, would consult Eamonn and his team at the National Museum Service. Thankfully I was now aware of the natural concerns of the licencing authorities and as a result I could provide greater detail in the relevant sections of the application to hopefully alleviate their concerns. He agreed that I could send him an early draft of my Method Statement for him to consider my approach in applying for this crucial licence. Here was a man who was encouraging me onwards. This was the shot in the arm I needed.

Although it seemed to be progress, it was still agonising watching the days drag by, waiting for some positive message to emanate from the authorities. Days turned to weeks. By now it was approaching the end of March. The Dublin archaeological authorities had a draft copy of my voluminous Method Statement to peruse. It set out concisely what we intended to do and how we were going to do it. They also had a copy of the GPR survey from Queens University Belfast plus letters of support from various authorities. I had also sent them letters from the MOD in relation to ownership issues and Derry City Council Heritage and Museum Services in relation to displaying any excavated remains. As requested, I had also retained the services of a suitably qualified archaeologist. Under the legislation, my Licence to Excavate application had to be submitted via a professional archaeologist.

After 3 weeks of relative silence, I received an email from Eamonn which indicated that 'things seemed in order' from his point of view. However he reiterated that the National Museum Service was just the consultation body in the issuing process, but that hopefully the DEHLG National Monument Service which issues the actual licences would concur. I formally declared a state of 'mild excitement' at this point and spent the next few nights and early mornings amending my Method Statement to clarify issues on which the Dublin authorities had requested further information.

At this point, I never wanted to see another application form for an archaeological licence for the rest of my life. It was therefore the cause of some mild distress when the archaeological authorities contacted me a few days later and informed me that I would be required to apply for a further licence – a Licence to Export! Apparently this was needed to legally remove any excavated archaeological remains from the Republic of Ireland into Northern Ireland. The aircraft remains would require immediate preservation once they were exposed to air, plus suitable and secure storage to safely undertake this work. As this was to be done at my home outside Derry, I had no other option but to add this required licence to my 'To Do' list.

After making all the required tweaks and alterations, on the 14th April, I formally submitted, via Ciara our archaeologist, two copies of my Method Statement plus their supporting Appendices. In terms of aviation archaeology, these documents represented my version of War and Peace. Blood, sweat and tears were distilled into every word. Like a father handing over a baby for adoption, I placed the documents into Ciara's hands and told her to look after them well as she prepared for them to go to Dublin where hopefully our application would be considered and determined within 3 - 4 weeks. In doing this, it seemed the weight of the world was lifted from my shoulders. There was nothing I could do now. It was down to the quality of my application and the decision makers. Instantaneously, the lifted weight was replaced with the weight of waiting.

CHAPTER 4

The Search for Bud's Family

It was very early in the project when my thoughts turned to the pilot and the possibility of tracing him. Documents from the Army Archive indicated Pilot Officer (P/O) Roland 'Bud' Wolfe was from Nebraska, USA and that he had been interned in the days after the crash. As my younger brother has lived in Nebraska for many years, I sounded him out for possible papers that could run a search campaign. I also asked my friend Brian York, who is the curator of the Strategic Air and Space Museum in Ashland, Nebraska for similar potential contacts. Both recommended the Omaha World Herald and one of its journalists called David Hendee.

Back at home, I was very fortunate to have access to the late Nat McGlinchey's files. Nat McGlinchey was a wonderful Eglinton man who, over many years, had diligently recorded the history of Eglinton Airport from its construction as a RAF fighter base through to the present day. For years he trawled the local newspapers for relevant articles which he meticulously filed away. He kept the lever arch file and poly-pocket manufacturers of the world in business. He used to call in with me for a 'quick chat' and soon an evening would pass as he recounted war time stories, local crashes and pilots he had met. He had practically spent all his school days on the wartime airfield and as a result he had the most incredible collection of stories, tales and acquaintances that a young schoolboy could ever want.

He told me he had corresponded with many of the Eglinton Eagle pilots and I recall him frequently mentioning Bud's name and his crash, but he never elaborated further on his relationship with him. Post war, Nat was made an honourary member of the Eagle Squadron Association for his efforts in keeping the 133 Eagle story alive in the Eglinton area. He always told me it was a shame there was no memorial to 133 Eagle Squadron at the City of Derry Airport and one day he was going to do something about it. Sadly he passed away before he had a chance to attend to this. I considered that if I ever had the chance to rectify this situation then Nat's name would certainly be on that plaque.

Nat's brother Brian kindly skimmed through some of Nat's files that he thought would be helpful and called me to let me know they were available. Not knowing what lay inside the dusty covers, I collected them and retired to my study for the evening. In Nat's yellowing files, I was immediately cast back to the early war time origins of the airfield. In the articles and photo's you could almost hear the sound of Merlin engines and smell the aviation fuel. Engrossed, I turned the pages and then, there it was – a letter from Bud Wolfe!

I sat up and stared down dumbstruck at the page. Up to this point I was researching a Spitfire with a pilot. The pilot had a name, but for whatever reason, the aircraft always seemed to be in the spotlight. Bud, up to this point, was always the understudy in this project. However from this moment onwards, things changed. As I excitedly flicked through successive pages, more and more letters in the same neat handwriting appeared, arranged by date and representing an exchange of letters between Nat and Bud that had gone on for several years during the late 80's and early 90's.

I won't go into the detail of the letters content as they were personal between Bud and Nat, but they provided me with a wealth of information about Bud's crash. He told Nat his recollections of the crash and knocked some rumours on the head. *I wasn't lost, my engine was boiling over* he stressed! Bud also recounted some brief thoughts on his days in the Curragh. He spoke of his post WW2 career with the US Air Force in the Korean and Vietnam conflicts and his civilian life, health and hobbies. He proudly spoke about his daughters, one of whom was serving in the US Air Force, and their careers. Each of the letters was affectionately signed 'Timber' which was apparently an old RAF nickname that Bud was happy for his friends to use. In all of the letters, he thanked Nat profusely for all the photographs and cuttings that he had sent over.

I turned to the very last letter in the file, dated April 1994, and immediately noticed it was in a different handwriting. The opening sentence thanked Nat for his condolences on the recent passing of Bud. The letter was from Bud's wife, Jerry. I had really hoped that I could have talked to the great man and told him what we were planning – but sadly it was too late. In her letter to Nat she referred to talk of a proposed 133 Squadron plaque, containing the names of the Eagles who had flown from there, being erected in the recently opened new terminal building. She asked if it went ahead, could she be sent a photo of it for her Memory Book. She added: *Bud would be so proud to know he was remembered that way!*

When reading these letters, I felt as if I was eavesdropping on these two friends. It was a unique insight into this war time crash. Up to this point, I had a few historical documents referring to the crash – the demise of P8074. Now in my hand, I was holding a series of handwritten letters from P/O Roland 'Bud' Wolfe to Nat who I had known for many years. I recalled my daughter Grace's reaction to the 'spooky' twist of fate that had occurred in McLaughlin's shop in Gleneely the previous month. Here was another quality spooky twist of fate. I wondered was I searching for this plane or was P8074 chasing me to ensure that the excavation happened.

I agonised over what to do with these letters. Should I use the addresses and information they contained to search for Bud's daughters? What would they think of the whole idea? Should I leave well alone? Eventually I concluded it would be the worst possible outcome that, if the dig went ahead, the family were to find out about it afterwards and were approached by journalists out of the blue for comment. I felt I owed it to their father's memory to courteously inform them of my intentions and take it a step at a time after that. An email was dispatched to the Omaha World Herald reporter, David Hendee, requesting if he could locate any family relatives of Bud in the Nebraska state area. A few weeks later he was back in touch. He had an address for one of Bud's daughters. He had traced them to the east coast of America, many hundreds of miles away from Nebraska and asked her if she would permit him to pass on her email address to me to explain my project. She agreed to this and I drafted a polite introductory email explaining who I was; what I was intending to do; the BBC NI programme background and basically left it at that. I did state that I fully appreciated my email may come as a bolt out of the blue and involved a sensitive and personal part of their father's career that they may not be fully au fait with. I also added if they didn't want to be involved in anyway, I would completely understand but I considered the Wolfe family required the courtesy of knowing.

A few days later, I received an email from Barbara Kurcharczyk. She explained her father had talked little of his WW2 flying career or his subsequent service flying fighter jets in Korea and Vietnam. She admitted my project, although intriguing, would require her and her other sister, Betty Wolfe, to reflect on her father's career. The potential for this part of his career, which he rarely discussed with his family, being told as part of a television programme also added another dimension which she would have to discuss with her sister. She graciously asked that she, Betty and the extended Wolfe family be allowed time to consider this project which could potentially open so many previously closed chapters in their lives in relation to their father. I explained that I had already gathered some historical documents in relation to her father's crash and shortly I was travelling to the Irish Defence Archive in Dublin to investigate numerous other files related to his crash and his time in the Curragh internment camp. I think Barbara appreciated my honesty at this stage and she agreed to discuss this over the next few weeks with her relatives and she would get back to me.

I am sure it was not an easy decision for a family to take a leap of faith with a complete stranger on the other side of the world. Discussing an unknown part of their father's life and with me holding all the information required considerable courage and trust. But slowly and surely over the forthcoming weeks, I corresponded with Betty and Barbara to fill them in on the details of this part of their father's WW2 career. We exchanged photographs and documents from our respective collections. They pointed me in the direction of the US Air Force Academy in Colorado where they had donated many of their father's war time photographs and documents. The Academy acts as the official document repository for the 3 Eagle Squadrons – the 71, 121 and Bud's 133 (Eagle) Squadrons RAF.

As our email relationship developed they eventually felt committed enough to send two heart warming letters of support to me for use in our final application package to the Dublin authorities. We had only been corresponding by email at this stage and I had not yet spoken to Betty and Barbara. This family was really trusting me from afar. I and the team were very moved by this support and became determined to deliver for them.

So what do we know about P/O Roland L 'Bud' Wolfe? My early research indicated a remarkable man, with an exemplary USAAF career and a stubborn reluctance to talk to his family about any of his war time exploits. He had flown in and survived 3 theatres of war – WW2, Korea and Vietnam. Even though one of his own daughters had forged a similarly successful career in the USAF, he still felt unwilling to share his experiences. This is not a unique situation. Many surviving veterans of WW2 feel either unwilling to, or unable to, discuss these events. *I was just doing my job* is a common quote from the survivors of this – quite possibly, our greatest generation. With Bud, this reluctance only appeared to soften when he fell in with old flying colleagues at reunions.

Bud was born on 12th January 1918 in McGehee, Arkansas and raised in the small town of Ceresco, Nebraska. He learnt to fly at Lincoln's Lindbergh Field in the late 1930's and he earned his commercial pilot rating in 1940 and flew for a living. He was a graduate of College View High School in Lincoln and briefly attended the University of Nebraska. His daughters described him as having a daredevil character with a desire from a young age for speed. There are many stories of motorbikes from his youth.

It was not surprising that with nearly 1000 flying hours, he was promptly accepted when he volunteered at the offices of the Clayton Knight Committee in Kansas in early 1941. This recruiting enterprise facilitated a supply via Canada of American volunteers to train as pilots for the RAF in case the war in Europe expanded. However as an American, volunteering to fly for the RAF was not straight forward. Bud was offering to assist the Allies before America officially entered the war in December 1941 after the Pearl Harbour attack. Up to this point, America had remained strictly neutral and had not involved itself in the war in Europe. Congress had passed strict neutrality acts in 1939 which prevented any recruitment in the United States (US) for service in the armed forces of a foreign government.

A presidential proclamation at the time had also forbid the use of a US passport to travel to a foreign country to enlist. After France fell in early 1940, the US relinquished strict enforcement of the provisions of the various neutrality acts, while still officially maintaining a neutral stance. The Clayton Knight Committee neatly sidestepped this neutrality issue by stating they were not specifically recruiting Americans to fight overseas, rather they facilitated a service which advised possible volunteers and enabled them to travel to Canada or England for training.

The US State Department also had a major concern in relation to the issue of US citizenship and Americans potentially signing up to fight for foreign powers. The 1907 Citizenship Act states: *'any American citizen shall be deemed to have expatriated himself when he has taken an oath of allegiance to any foreign state.'* Eventually, following discussions between the British and Canadian governments, a typical Clayton Knight Committee solution was found whereby Americans volunteers who entered either the Royal Canadian Air Force or the RAF swore to obey the orders of their commanders, without having to swear allegiance to the king.

Not put off by these US neutrality legalities and potential risks to his citizenship Bud, having passed his selection interview, later took a 30 minute flight to demonstrate his flying proficiency. Even after this, Bud was still not guaranteed to be selected. A confidential report was then prepared on each candidate by a private investigation firm. Despite the urgent need for pilots, the Clayton Knight Committee accepted only about 6,700 pilots from among nearly 50,000 applicants.

Bud was one of the most experienced pilots to join the Eagle Squadrons. He was sent to the RAF Refresher Training Programme at Love Field in Dallas. Bud completed his training there in May 1941 and next went to Canada. On 5th June 1941, he was commissioned as a pilot officer in the RAF Volunteer Reserve and sailed for England. On arrival in England, he officially signed in with the Air Ministry in London and got himself measured up for his various uniform requirements, before moving to the 3 Personnel Reception Centre at Bournemouth.

He reported to 56 Operational Training Unit at Sutton Bridge in July where he learnt to fly the Hawker Hurricane and received an introduction in combat training. After successfully completing this training, he was assigned to 133 Squadron at Duxford, just south of Cambridge on 25th August 1941 as part of the original composition of this squadron. In early October, possibly as a result of several accidents, the squadron was sent to RAF Eglinton, some 7 miles northeast of Derry, for further training. They departed Duxford in their Hurricanes on the 8th October. 15 aircraft took off with a planned refuelling stop scheduled for Andreas airfield on the Isle of Man. However the weather deteriorated rapidly and thick cloud descended almost to ground level. One pilot turned back, while ten, including Bud, managed to get down at various airfields across the Isle of Man through a small break in the clouds. Unfortunately 4 experienced pilots were the victims of the atrocious weather; three were found dead in their wrecked aircraft scattered across the island's rocky mountainside and one aircraft and its pilot simply vanished and was never found.

The surviving pilots arrived in Eglinton on the 11th October and were none too happy with their new airfield which was still under construction. One squadron member described it as a *'vast sea of mud surrounded by knee deep lakes of mud and water'*. While in Eglinton the squadron was re-equipped with Spitfire Mk IIa's. They spent their time familiarising themselves with this new fighter and flying convoy patrols out over the North Atlantic – an inhospitable environment.

Nearby Derry offered a break to the fliers to socialise. The war had transformed the strategically vital port of Derry into a boom-town. At any one time 20,000 sailors were present. The competition for female company was therefore fierce but one seldom saw an Eagle pilot alone. One of their favourite watering holes was the Northern Counties Club in Bishop Street. They were also fond of partying hard in the Officers Mess on the airfield. The squadron diary records things getting slightly out of hand during the 1941 Christmas party. When the rationed coal ran out, they chopped up the Christmas tree and soaked it in aviation fuel. The subsequent fire engulfed the Mess and the station fire brigade and engines from Eglinton, Derry and Limavady were needed to douse the flames. On January 31st 1941, 133 Squadron departed to Kirton in Lindsey, an RAF airfield 15 miles north of Lincoln, England. All that is with the exception of Bud Wolfe.

A secret war time agreement between the British Government's representative Sir John Maffey and Eire's Taoiseach Eamonn de Valera was made in late January 1941 and allowed Allied aircraft to enter Irish airspace and fly across a portion of the 'Free State', as the Irish Republic was then known. This agreement gave the Allies a direct westerly flight out of their new flying boat bases in Northern Ireland at Lough Erne, Co Fermanagh and into the Atlantic to hunt the U-boats and protect convoys bringing essential supplies from America to Britain. Prior to this agreement, aircraft going on patrol from these bases had to fly north over Northern Ireland until they reached the coast before then heading west out into the Atlantic. This wasted time and valuable fuel, thereby limiting their hunting and protecting range.

Two corridors were agreed, Route A and Route B. Route A was a four mile corridor that ran between the flying boat bases in Fermanagh in Northern Ireland and Ballyshannon in Co. Donegal. The longer Route B ran northwards from Fermanagh over Northern Ireland before entering Irish airspace in Co Donegal and crossing the coast at Malin Head, Ireland's most northerly point. It was this Route B that was regularly used by the RAF fighters at Eglinton and the Coastal Command bombers that were based at airfields at Ballykelly and Limavady, along the Northern Ireland edge of Lough Foyle. Spitfires only had a limited range of about 450 miles. The availability of this corridor across neutral Eire allowed the Eagle squadron to take off from Eglinton and fly over Lough Foyle before cutting directly across the hills of the Inishowen Peninsula and straight into the north Atlantic to begin their convoy patrols.

While undertaking one of these routine but dangerous convoy patrols on the 30th November 1941, Bud noticed his engine temperature gauge was rapidly climbing. Knowing his engine wouldn't last much longer, Bud left the patrol and headed directly due south for RAF Eglinton by flying over the Inishowen peninsula through the permitted Route B corridor. However it soon became apparent to Bud that, despite being agonisingly close to home, he could coax no more life out of his Rolls Royce Merlin engine. If it had powered him on for just a further 3 minutes, he could have made it home. To add insult to injury his radio transmitter developed a fault at the same time. He could transmit messages, which were being heard at RAF Eglinton, but he could not receive any messages they were sending him. His last reported words received at Eglinton were *I'm going over the side!*

Shortly before 12 30pm, with his base within sight, Bud reluctantly executed a text book bale out. He took off his helmet and oxygen mask and set them over his gun sight directly in front of him in the cockpit. He released his Sutton harness, slid back the perspex cockpit canopy, opened the side door on the port side of his Spitfire and launched himself into the air over the cold and foggy Inishowen peninsula.

Witnesses recall seeing his abandoned aircraft screaming out of the low cloud and burying itself in the soft peat bog in the hills above Gleneely. At more than 350mph, it took a ¼ of a second for the Spitfire to disappear 30ft beneath the moor.

Having parachuted safely, a member of Ireland's Local Defence Force apprehended Bud near Moneydarragh, and Ireland added him to a growing population of detained Allied personnel – mostly aviators and German U-boat crewmen and Luftwaffe aircrew who also ended up on neutral Irish soil during the early years of the war.

So he ended up in prison for the rest of the war – what a cracking story I thought. In the weeks ahead, I was to discover that in reality, I didn't know the half of it.

CHAPTER 5

Things Get Better and Better

It is often said that the eye of a hurricane is calm and serene and controls the path of the storm, while around it, chaos and destruction reign. I could possibly use this analogy for the controlling role of producer John Hayes Fisher as Dig WW2 raged around him. For it was he who had the unenviable role of allocating a significant portion of his production budget in filming the three proposed aviation digs to feature in the series. He had to take the risk of committing to follow the various excavations the aviation team were suggesting to undertake. And here I was, suggesting to him that he may get a good story if he took a leap of faith with me and my potentially hare brained scheme to excavate a buried plane from a deep bog.

Bud's dig, if it ever went ahead, was to be a 5-6 minute feature in one of the hour long Dig WW2 episodes. All John wanted to do was tag along at each of our digs, document the story behind each crash and then film how we went about excavating the aircraft. He also wanted to portray how military archaeology differs from conventional archaeology and also the growing reality that sadly we only have a few more years at most to actually speak to these now elderly pilots and aircrew who participated in WW2. Accordingly, seeking out and interviewing such individuals was a priority, as was researching their background story and compiling any supporting historic documents to complement their story in the series.

When I rang to tell him that Grace and I had found P8074, he was mildly relieved but slightly concerned about its location in a bog. This excavation should it go ahead he reckoned would just be a 'stocking filler' in the first episode. Nothing to get excited about in the whole scale of things.

Then I rang him to say I had been to the actual site and had seen small bits of the aircraft. Now he could potentially begin to firm up the inclusion of this aircraft in the series. Slightly stressed John became more happy John. Then the licencing fun and games began. All our digs are done legally and this one, despite the significant paperwork that it seemed to entail, would be no different. I kept John up to speed with my licencing woes, explaining that the entire process showed every indication of it being a long, drawn out process.

John and I kept in regular contact as I navigated my way through the licencing complexities from the Dublin authorities. He used his contacts with the National Museum to assure them that we intended to undertake this project in strict accordance with the legislation. Out of this came order and soon between himself, myself and the authorities, we had developed a list of requirements that needed to be ticked to progress towards securing the relevant licences. Happily this resulted in the uncertainty I faced being removed and replaced with a long uphill slog of typing to produce a bespoke Method Statement for the first licenced excavation of a war time aircraft in Ireland, North or South.

With the project now apparently progressing down a defined route that hopefully would lead to licencing happiness, I was now able to relax to a degree in relation to my paperwork issues. I began to focus on Bud Wolfe himself. What info could I bring to John to include in the series? How much information did he need for a 5 or 6 minute story? Was there really a story to be told other than 'Bud crashed his plane?'

In the days and weeks ahead, I busied myself on accurately researching Bud's career through historical documents and photographs. These are the sort of things that producers like to see to and put in front of the camera to bring the story to life. John was a producer and not an aviation enthusiast. He needed the information to be well researched, supported with contemporaneous documents and presented in a way that people would easily understand. I don't mean this in a cruel way, but the intended target audience of the series would not all be aviation fanatics either. The stories to feature in the series needed to appeal to a wide audience and grip the viewers' imagination.

So far, John was happy with the information I had supplied him with. He could tell the story of the young Nebraskan pilot who had volunteered to fly with an RAF Eagle squadron before America formally entered the War.

The Eagles had been temporarily based in Eglinton, Northern Ireland. It ticked all the Dig WW2 boxes.

Then things escalated. My earlier research revealed that Bud had been interned in neutral Ireland in the Curragh Camp, Co Kildare for several years. I though it wise to look into this a bit more. In the days ahead I was to be left open mouthed as I investigated the facts behind Bud's internment. After he had parachuted to safety on the 30th November 1941, Bud unfortunately remained in the Moneydarragh countryside, keen to get to his crashed aircraft. A local Moneydarragh myth persists that he was keen to retrieve a valuable watch that he had left in the cockpit of his Spitfire. A tall, American pilot carrying a parachute through Moneydarragh was not hard to miss and he was soon apprehended in Moneydarragh at 1 30 pm by a Mr William Doran of the Local Defence Force and taken to Moville Garda station. He was handed over to Lt Crawford at 6 pm and accommodated in the Irish Army barracks at Rockhill, Letterkenny that night. He was taken to Athlone on 1st Dec 1941 and sent to the internment camp in the Curragh on the same day.

Once there, the senior English RAF officers quickly tried to impress on the young American the need to observe the parole system in operation in the camp. Parole was a conditional release from the confines of the camp. It was a privilege granted by the Camp Command to both the Allied and German internees alike. Having signed a parole form, individuals were permitted to leave the camp, but stay within a radius of 10 miles, until 2 am every day of the week. However it was an enforced code of RAF honour that deterred individuals from signing out and walking to the border.

Once a parole slip had been signed it was an indication of the individual, as an officer and a gentleman of the RAF, that they would honour the terms and spirit of the parole system. It was an unwritten rule that individuals must return to the camp otherwise they would seen as having brought dishonour to themselves, their country and the RAF who had agreed to honour this system. However once an individual's parole was cancelled on his return to camp, he was perfectly entitled to escape with the full approval of the RAF. The unwritten code of conduct also forbid officers from planning escapes, talking about escapes or enlisting help to escape from the surrounding community while on parole.

This went down like a lead balloon with Bud who had enlisted because of his love of flying fast fighters. He had little desire to spend his time behind the wires in this strange form of open prison. A week later the Japanese attacked Pearl Harbour in Hawaii. Bud's spirits rose as he anticipated an enraged America entering the war. He was bound to be released soon he thought. Over the days ahead, this optimism declined. He realised as 1941 came to a close that although the Germans were not winning the war, neither sadly were the Alllies. The Americans entering the war was not going to provide an immediate solution. So while Pearl Harbour had provided him with a temporary shot in the arm, he quickly realised that the RAF were going to need his services. He had to escape!

On Friday 13th December, Bud met with a fellow 133 Squadron flier from RAF Eglinton. Flying Officer (F/O) Johnny Jackson had been granted permission to travel to the Curragh to bring down some of Bud's clothing and toiletries. What happened over the following hours is still the subject of great controversy. The Irish authorities, the RAF and the American Minister to Ireland all dispute the various versions of events and the implications of Bud's actions.

The facts as can best be ascertained are as follows. Bud and F/O Jackson left the camp shortly after 4pm, Bud having signed a parole form indicating he would be back at 2am at the latest. They headed to the nearby town of Naas for dinner and a few drinks. When the pair returned to the main gate at 10 30 pm, earlier than planned, they found the police hut unattended. Bud quickly realised he had been presented with the chance he needed to re-enter the war. Leaving F/O Jackson at the main gate, Bud walked back into the camp and after a few minutes returned to the empty police hut. There, he took a blank parole form and signed himself out for his second parole of the day and walked towards the guards and F.O. Jackson at the main gate. So far, Bud was fulfilling all the rules of parole. At the main gate, the guards inspected Bud's parole form. He indicated he was heading out for a last drink with his squadron friend before Jackson returned to Eglinton. The guards waved the pair through the gates. Now it becomes complicated.

A few steps beyond the gate, Bud turned and asked the guards could he return for a pair of gloves. Not an unreasonable request for anyone in the middle of December to ask. The guards agreed this would be no problem and minutes after starting this second parole, Bud left Jackson at the gate again and returned to his hut for his gloves. Technically at this point Bud was still on parole having signed a parole slip indicating he would be back before 2am. He walked back from his hut with his gloves to the police hut and found it still empty. He took his second parole slip for this nightcap drink and stamped it 'Cancelled' and left it in the tray. The logic in Bud's thinking was that he had officially returned to camp to fulfil the obligations of his second parole that evening. He equated returning to camp as returning from beyond the camp gates and past the guards for his gloves. Seeing Bud approach with his gloves, the two guards waved him on through the gates. His parole cancelled, Bud had effectively been allowed to walk out through the Curragh gates without any insistence that he sign a third parole slip. He considered he had legitimately escaped as he was not subject of any parole restrictions. The pair headed to Dublin, caught the morning train to Belfast and that afternoon were both back in RAF Eglinton where Bud became the subject of an intense international diplomatic storm.

At the highest level, a war of words erupted between the British representative to Eire, the RAF air attaché in Dublin and the American Minister to Ireland. At a meeting convened at the Curragh, at which all the Allied internees were present, the British representative Sir John Maffey was very insistent that Bud had escaped unlawfully. His actions were the subject of an investigation and it was highly likely he would be returned. He insisted that Wolfe's conduct was hardly becoming an RAF officer. Maffey also hinted that the Irish authorities were seriously considering withdrawing the parole system which was enjoyed by all the Allied internees. Rousing the crowd, he stressed that Bud's actions were going to seriously impact on the quality of life they enjoyed in the Curragh. It was the spirit and not the legal interpretation of the parole system he emphasised to the officers. Bud's good name as an officer and a gentleman was being called into dispute. A week later Bud was returned to the Curragh on the instructions of the Air Ministry in London.

However, the escape known diplomatically as the 'Wolfe affair' was now under scrutiny from David Grey, the American Minister to Ireland. Determined to safeguard Bud's honour, he fully investigated all the facts behind the escape and interviewed all the relevant camp personnel. His investigation revealed that the camp authorities were very embarrassed about the police hut being left unmanned. They also disputed Bud's version of events based on the testimonies of the two gate guards. The guards denied Bud had returned momentarily into the camp for a pair of gloves – effectively fooling them. They insisted Bud had signed a new parole slip and then just walked out of the camp and travelled back to Eglinton. Their version of events was relayed as the truth to the senior RAF officer in charge of the internees and was later used by the RAF as the basis of their reasoning to force Bud to return to the Curragh. Grey's investigation cast doubt over the gate guards' version of events and subsequently undermined the reasoning used by the RAF to return Bud from Eglinton.

He subsequently prepared a report and met the Irish Taoiseach Eamon de Valera on 23rd February at which he asked de Valera to reverse the RAF decision and release Bud. This request was refused.

Grey in his report stated:
Senior RAF officers at the camp, having been made aware of the full facts behind the manner of Bud's leaving, now believe Wolfe's version of the escape as did Air Officers in the Squadron stationed in Northern Ireland. It was realised that in returning Wolfe, the Air Ministry had acted on a point of honour in the light of the information then available to them and that the information now available required that action to be set aside.

He concluded:
With the direct testimony of two American officers serving in the RAF explicitly alleging that Pilot Officer Wolfe returned a third time within the compound and went out without signing a new parole, I feel called upon, at the least, to take such action as will bring the available supporting evidence before Pilot Officer Wolfe's superiors and to make such report to the Department of State as will tend to safeguard his honour as an officer and a gentleman.

Bud's return indicated to the internees, that despite the Americans entering the war, there was going to be no immediate release for them. In time most of them agreed and supported Wolfe's justification for his escape. A few of the English RAF officers upset at their temporary loss of parole during the 'Wolfe affair' engaged Bud in fisticuffs. Bud had been a keen boxer during his school days in Nebraska and always gave a good account of himself. Eventually the whole affair blew over and Bud settled himself into the Curragh way of life again. Frequent parties, golfing and hunting trips were the norm. Eventually Bud and the other officers were released when the camp closed in October 1943.

This aspect of Bud's career now gave the programme the opportunity to intertwine the story of neutral Ireland during the war, the subject of internment to consider; an escape route to retrace and an international row to analyse. You think the producer would be happy. "How am I to fit this all in?" he frequently moaned. Producers can be so ungrateful.

Further research uncovered more and more fascinating elements to Bud's career. These discoveries were playing havoc with the timings of the first episode of Dig WW2. I emailed John to let him know that Bud, after his release from the internment camp in 1943, was transferred to the US Army Air Force and resumed flying. He survived WW2 and later flew with the US Air Force when it became a separate service in 1947. He flew jets fighters in both the Korean and Vietnam wars and retired as the base commander in Vietnam. He amassed nearly 12,000 flying hours and flew 847 combat missions during three wars which is considered possibly a record for a US pilot. The original 5 or 6 minute Bud Wolfe story was now edging towards the half hour mark. Episode 1 of Dig WW2 was rapidly becoming 'The Story of Bud Wolfe'.

It was important in telling the story that there were examples of historical documents to intersperse with the footage of the excavation. So in early May Chris Nikkel, the 360 Production researcher on the story, and myself headed to the Irish Military Archives in the Cathal Brugha Barracks in Dublin. Prior to our arrival the Archive staff assembled 9 boxes containing all the war time official letters on the crash. There were also copies of Bud's personal RAF documents and a host of other relevant bits and pieces.

It was an incredible few hours; a real privilege to sit and read these personal letters, to look at Bud's signature on a parole form and read the musty, yellowing Army Intelligence file on the crash. In amongst the general pages of internment documents, we found Bud's RAF identity card and then perhaps the most emotional direct link to Bud. It was an internment camp copy of a handwritten letter from Bud, written a few days after the crash, to his father in Nebraska. In it, he apologised to his father for any distress his crash caused the Wolfe family and joked about the slight international incident he had created. He then ended the letter by asking his father to send him some warm jumpers as his camp was bitterly cold and windy.

We scanned these letters and many more documents to ensure the Bud Wolfe story would be credibly and fully supported with historical evidence. I stepped out of the Archive and rang John who was, at that moment, walking around the Curragh camp investigating possible shoot locations. I updated him on the wealth of relevant information we had found. I think at this point he realised the game was up and the Bud Wolfe story was going to be the star of the series and accordingly would require a serious amount of screen time.

"It's an incredible story" John admitted, "I can't imagine how it could get any better".

A few days later, I rang John's mobile.
"Hello John, its Jonny...it's about the Donegal Spitfire story....there's been a development ...I'm afraid it has just got better."

After a long pause, he asked how and I quickly rattled through the facts.

"Garfield Weston was a very successful Canadian retail mogul and philanthropist. During WW2 he made a single donation of £100,000 to the Wings for Britain Fund in August 1940 to pay for the replacement of 16 Spitfires that had been lost in a single battle"

"Go on" said John.

"He bought 8 new Spitfires and 6 Hurricanes in a gesture that captivated the newspapers and spurred on a frenzy of public donating. Each of the

Spitfires he presented was painted with his name down the side of the fuel tank, just in front of the cockpit and ours…"

More silence from John.

"And our Spitfire P8074 was the very first one he donated! It's 'Garfield Weston 1' I've just spoken to the Weston Foundation's archive people in Toronto and they are very excited – very excited indeed!"

And if you listened very closely to the phone, you could hear the sound of the Dig WW2 script being ripped up and fluttering through the air

CHAPTER 6

The Garfield Weston Connection

The Garfield Weston connection lifted this otherwise 1940 standard Supermarine Spitfire Mk IIa, made at the Castle Bromwich factory, into the fighter Hall of Fame. It bestowed a status on P8074 that gave it a truly global appeal and ensured that this was going to be a far from quiet little excavation, if and when it happened. The Weston name was synonymous with the establishment of the WW2 Spitfire Funds which enabled a beleaguered British public to donate money towards the purchase of much needed aircraft, including the iconic Spitfires and Hurricanes. In this way, aircraft named after the individuals, streets or companies that collected a token £5,000, which purchased the basic shell and engine of a Spitfire, could personally take the fight to Hitler and his Luftwaffe. But what was behind this very successful man and responsible for the purchase of this fighter and 13 others? Biscuits!

Willard Garfield Weston was born in 1898 in Toronto. His father George ran a successful bread factory in the city. Before joining the Canadian Expeditionary Force and fighting in World War 1, he served his time on the factory floor learning how to maintain the equipment. He returned from France in 1919 and began his ascent up the Weston factory management ladder. He rapidly expanded the family business, acquiring other bakery and biscuit factories, particularly during the Great Depression of the early 1930's. Having successfully entered the United Kingdom market in the mid 1930's, he decided he would have to move the Weston family, eventually comprising 9 children, from Canada to England in order to manage his burgeoning empire.

While undoubtedly achieving great success in business, Garfield Weston also had a great interest in politics. In November 1939, two months after Britain declared war on Hitler and Nazi Germany; he became the MP for Macclesfield. However it is not for his actions in the House of Commons that he is remembered. He rose to prominence for his philanthropic work and rallying cries to the Empire, particularly to his fellow Canadians, to assist the war effort.

He donated 500 radios after the first contingent of Canadian troops to arrive in England complained of boredom while restricted to camp. He lent his name and support to a Tank Fund. During the Blitz, he set up a canteen operation in the London Underground to feed an estimated 150,000 civilians a night, who attempted to seek safety in the depths away from the nightly German aerial bombing campaign.

He was even involved in a clandestine mission, under orders from Churchill, to attempt to persuade the steadfastly neutral Irish state to open her ports and harbours to the British Navy to facilitate refuelling, supplies and repairs. Although an agreement was reached with the Irish Government the American President, when informed of the brokered deal, demanded it be stopped to prevent a feared negative reaction from Irish Americans which could cost him his re-election.

After the war, Garfield Weston returned to Canada and further business success and in 1959, he and his wife Rena established the Garfield Weston Charitable Foundation. A son, Willard Galen Weston, is the executive chairman of George Weston Limited and Holt Renfrew in Canada and the Selfridges Group in the UK. He is also the Chairman of the W Garfield Weston Foundation which has made close to $200 million in donations over the past decade. Galen Weston had been alerted to our proposed project by the Weston archivist during my research with him and was very excited to hear about our proposed project and asked to be kept updated. His father's war time donation of aircraft in 1940, when he was less than a year old, is still considered by the Weston family to be a very significant and emotional event. Galen Weston's personal assistant told me the dig could potentially unearth parts of one of these Spitfires and 70 years later re-connect Mr Weston with a tangible part of his father's war time exploits. No pressure there then!

However it is the £100,000 donation to the Ministry of Aircraft production in August 1940 which is the most well known of his war effort contributions and directly relevant to the story of P8074. The gifting of weapons during times of war is an age old practice but it was brought to the fore during World War 1, when the Nizam of Hyderabad, one of the richest rulers in India, donated a sum of money that enabled the British Royal Flying Corps, which later became the RAF in 1919, to purchase an entire squadron of fighters which were named after him in honour of his generous gift. Interestingly this was 152 Squadron, and it was their Spitfire BM557 that I had been searching for at the City of Derry Airport, Eglinton without any success since the early 1990's before switching my attention to the Donegal hills and P8074. In 1939 the Nizam donated another £100,000 and in so doing created the Wings for Britain Fund.

In August 1940, Garfield Weston turned up at the offices of an exhausted, Lord Beaverbrook who was a fellow Canadian. He was the Minister for Aircraft Production and he had just received news that 16 RAF fighters had been lost in a single battle. The figure of 16 was released at the time as the number of aircraft reportedly lost in action on the 18th August. Weston was reported to have said to Beaverbrook, who allegedly broke down at the gesture: *Sadly I can't replace these brave young men, but I can replace the aircraft.* He handed over a blank cheque which Beaverbrook filled in for £100,000, adding that Weston's donation would raise many times more money. Weston was particularly close to the brave British and Canadian pilots who risked their lives day and night. He frequently offered his family estate at Wittington, outside London to Canadian Army, Navy and Air Force personnel as a retreat while on their service leave.

The gesture made front page news across the papers next day and it ignited the public imagination to fund raising and donating to the Wings for Britain Fund. Eventually the Wings for Britain Fund raised enough money to pay for more than 2,200 assorted aircraft, including some 1,600 Spitfires. Having donated the money to purchase the basic airframe, from £5,000 for a fighter to £20,000 for a four engined heavy bomber, the aircraft carried a relevant name chosen by its sponsor. Garfield Weston's donation enabled the funding of 16 fighters, initially 8 Spitfires and then later on 6 Hurricanes. Each of the Weston Spitfires carried the name Garfield Weston painted onto the port (left) side of the fuel tank cowling, located just in front of the cockpit.

After the Weston name, to distinguish the aircraft, they carried a letter S (for Spitfire) and then roman numerals I through to IIX. P8074 was the first of the 8 and the name 'Garfield Weston S I' was duly applied to it in RAF standard sea grey paint in two inch tall letters over the standard dark earth / dark green camouflage scheme.

This donation soon inspired further sizable donations from other wealthy sources, in particular a donation of $1 million from Canadian J. W. McConnell, the publisher of the Montreal Star and yet another £100,000 from the Nizam of Hyderabad. At a time of great financial hardship for many, the public responded to these donations by organising their own fund raising efforts and soon Spitfire Funds had been set up the length and breadth of the country.

In Northern Ireland the Belfast Telegraph Spitfire Appeal Fund, launched in August 1940, raised over £90,000 – enough to buy 17 Spitfires. Lord Beaverbrook applauded the effort saying: *There was never anything anywhere like the Belfast Telegraph Spitfire Appeal Fund.* All 17 Spitfires, named after Northern Ireland towns and counties, saw active service but sadly none survived the war. In all 12 pilots were die at the controls of these donated aircraft, including Sgt Pilot A Taylor (New Zealand) in 'City of Derry'. A similar fate befell all the Weston Spitfires. All succumbing to crashes or being struck of charge and scrapped before the end of WW2.

Days after making the donation, Garfield Weston made a broadcast over the BBC and Canadian Broadcasting Channel (CBC). In a stirring speech made to ignite the funding fires of his homeland and the Empire, Weston proclaimed nothing less than the future of civilization was at stake:

"In the stillness of the night, this message rings out to all mankind: 'This nation has been chosen by a living God to defend the rights of men. It cannot fail!!' And the echoes come back from all parts of the Empire: 'It cannot fail! It cannot fail! It cannot fail!'

With Garfield Weston's rallying cry echoing in my ears, I began to ponder the odds of my project actually happening. There was still no official word back from the Dublin authorities, but that didn't overly concern me. What began to worry me was the logistics and cost of the actual excavation if they gave it the go ahead. It would take the definition of being gutted to a new level, if I was given permission to dig but then found out in reality I actually couldn't.

What if all the potential contractors, having viewed the site, were not willing to risk their expensive diggers in the bog or the costs involved for those willing to give it a try were too prohibitive?

With that in mind, I began looking for a willing digger firm. A quick look through the phone book identified several prospective contractors. Family and friends suggested other digger companies. I needed a firm who had a long reach digger capable of digging a hole to a depth of 40ft. These diggers come in a variety of weights. I wanted a light one, around the 20 / 22 ton mark. I wanted a firm who had experience of soft ground operation – very, very soft ground operation! It would also be a bonus if they were based a stone's throw away from the crash site to keep the transport costs down.

It quickly became apparent that only a few firms in NI had these kinds of diggers and the necessary experience. In turn they visited the crash site and said it was possible to get diggers to the crash site, but after that the sums varied wildly as they each differed on the amount of ground preparation needed to get their machinery safely to the actual crash site. Some contractors wanted to lay a road right down to the crater, while others wanted to skim off all the bog vegetation to reach a more solid level. Another issue was that most were based many miles away from the crash site and accordingly transport costs were very significant. Producer John had a small budget set aside for assisting with each excavation to feature in the series, but he quickly realised that given the terrific story surrounding this aircraft, his proposed budget wasn't going to be anywhere near what I needed. Accordingly he had to 'tweak' his figures.

Then I remembered something Martin Kearney told me on the day when we found the crash site in February. After I rang him to tell him we had pinpointed the impact crater, he said: "Sure, if you need a digger man to dig it out, my brother Danny has a digger firm. He doesn't live too far away."

One night in early spring, I met Danny on the mountain and we walked down to the crash site. While other contractors and their assistants who had come out to look at the site had slipped and stumbled over the bog, frequently commenting how wet it was, Danny strode sure footed and spoke quietly.

He looked and measured and estimated with an experienced eye that had seen these sorts of locations before. It was all very straight forward he considered. A couple of diggers, one being a long reach, a few bog mats to sit the diggers on, a bit of safety fencing and possibly a pump if the hole threatened to flood. His understated style of delivery hid a considerable experience of undertaking years of soft ground work. He was local, he knew the mountain from his youth, and he was the brother of the man who helped me find the aircraft. It appeared that the special brand of Moneydarragh fate was up to her old tricks again.

We discussed the proposed plan. Producer John wanted the team on the moor for 8am on dig day to start filming various pieces to camera. The diggers would need to be in place at the crash site the day before to facilitate this. The diggers would need to fill in the hole on the day of the dig, reinstate the moor surface and vegetation afterwards and put up a protective fence around the infilled crater. In essence we were looking at a three day project. The digger needed to have the reach to ensure that it could dig down to retrieve the aircraft's engine, estimated to be buried 30ft beneath the surface. As the ground conditions were waterlogged, it was a distinct possibility that the sides of the hole could slump and collapse as we dug down. The extra reach on a long armed digger meant we could have the digger sitting well back from the crater sides should this start to happen.

The digger also needed the power to lift a 650 kg Merlin engine from such a depth. Unfortunately such power only came in the heavier long reach diggers. Heavy diggers, deep wet bogs – it had potential disaster written all over it.

As we walked off the mountain in the evening twilight, Danny asked did many people watch these sorts of programmes. I informed him the last series 'Dig 1940' attracted 4 million viewers. Without showing the slightest concern at such figures, he added in all seriousness, that he would wash his diggers for the big day if he got the job.

Roland 'Bud' Wolfe
in his RAF Eagle Squadron uniform.
Photo courtesy of
USAFA McDermott Library SMS 1090.

One of the 8 Weston presentation Spitfires – P8084 – Garfield Weston VI.
Photo courtesy of The Weston Corporate Archives.

Local knowledge indicated the crash site lay somewhere towards the top of this gully.

The team head off to search the gully. Little did we know, P8074 actually lay beneath the photographer's feet. *Photo courtesy of Damien Gallagher.*

Early investigations after getting strong readings from the magnetometer.
Photo courtesy of Damien Gallagher.

I can feel metal! *Photo courtesy of Damien Gallagher.*

This piece of shiny aluminium still retaining its wartime camouflage confirmed we had found the impact point. *Photo courtesy of Damien Gallagher.*

The team standing in the impact crater discussing what to do next.
Photo courtesy of Damien Gallagher.

The diggers performing the bog-mat waltz.

Serious excavations require serious machinery.
Photo courtesy of Jacinta Melaugh.

"So you tell me there's a Spitfire beneath my feet?"
Photo courtesy of Jacinta Melaugh.

The first Browning machine gun of the day. *Photo courtesy of Jacinta Melaugh.*

Soon we were finding significant quantities of
.303 ammunition.
Photo courtesy of Jacinta Melaugh.

A happy Glyn with
another Browning.
*Photo courtesy of
Jacinta Melaugh.*

Ordnance Corps technicians go to work. *Photo courtesy of Jacinta Melaugh.*

Even after 70 years, the bullets were in immaculate condition.
Photo courtesy of Jacinta Melaugh.

The base of a shattered propeller blade was a significant early find.
Photo courtesy of Jacinta Melaugh.

At about 12ft, the peat gave way to sticky blue clay.
Photo courtesy of Jacinta Melaugh.

A typical Donegal summer's day – a mix of bright sunshine and low black clouds. *Photo courtesy of Jacinta Melaugh.*

And the occasional torrential downpour. *Photo courtesy of Jacinta Melaugh.*

As the hole deepens, we gather round the bucket to inspect the finds.
Photo courtesy of Jacinta Melaugh.

The tail wheel assembly moments after it was recovered.
Photo courtesy of Jacinta Melaugh.

The digger was now recovering serious quantities of wreckage.
Photo courtesy of Jacinta Melaugh.

Soon the site was a hive of activity. *Photo courtesy of Jacinta Melaugh.*

The moment we found the Garfield Weston stencilled piece.
Photo courtesy of Jacinta Melaugh.

Dan proudly holds aloft Bud Wolfe's flying helmet. *Photo courtesy of Jacinta Melaugh.*

From 33ft down, the iconic Rolls Royce Merlin engine sees the light of day again.
Photo courtesy of Jacinta Melaugh.

A good day in the office! *Photo courtesy of Jacinta Melaugh.*

The still inflated rear tail wheel.
Photo courtesy of Jacinta Melaugh.

The shattered blade reunited with the propeller hub.
Photo courtesy of Jacinta Melaugh.

Filling in the hole at the end of an incredible day. *Photo courtesy of Jacinta Melaugh.*

The Merlin after a long steam clean. *Photo courtesy of Damien Gallagher*

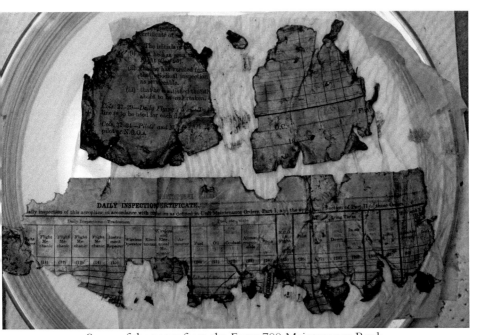

Some of the pages from the Form 700 Maintenance Book.
Photo courtesy of Damien Gallagher

A selection of cleaned cockpit dials and instruments including the blind flying panel (rear) and part of the gun sight (front).

The flying helmet with part of the frame of Bud's flying goggles.

Dylan holding the port fuselage RAF roundel.

The tail wheel touches down with Grace's
help on the Eglinton runway.
*Photo courtesy of Martin McKeown
- Inpresspics.com*

Mr and Mrs Galen Weston, author Dr Jonathan Vance and myself in Toronto with the piece of fuel tank cowling bearing Garfield Weston's name.

Mr Galen Weston with the piece of his father's presentation Spitfire.

Final checks before firing.

"Dylan cannot attend school today as he is firing WW2 machine guns".

Col Gerald Aherne and Lt Col Dave Sexton with Dylan and myself on the firing range in Athlone. We presented them with a polished cog taken from the Merlin engine.
Photo courtesy of Paul Molloy

Barbara, Betty, extended family and friends attend a short commemorative service at the site, 70 years to the very hour of the crash.

Photo courtesy of Derry Journal Newspapers

Barbara views the display case at the City of Derry Airport.
Photo courtesy of Chris Craig.

The Wolfe family, Mayor Alderman Maurice Devenney and the management of the City of Derry Airport at the unveiling of the plaque and display case.
Photo courtesy of Chris Craig.

Barbara and Betty with the Mayor and Roisin Doherty (Head of Heritage and Museum Service, Derry City Council) when they visited the Guildhall.
Photo courtesy of Keith Moore, Londonderry Sentinel.

Betty admires one of the Browning machine guns on display in the Workhouse Museum.
Photo courtesy of Photo courtesy of Martin McKeown - Inpresspics.com

The pilot's oxygen supply cockpit dials as displayed in the museum.
Photo courtesy of Martin McKeown - Inpresspics.com

The launch of the P8074 story at the Workhouse Museum.
Photo courtesy of Martin McKeown - Inpresspics.com

CHAPTER 7

"I'm Finding it Difficult to Contain Myself!"

It was now mid May and there was still no word from the authorities in Dublin. I had to state a date range for the proposed dig on the excavation licence application and I had indicated the end of June as my preferred time. This suited the team, the production company and most of the diggers firms that had visited the site to prepare quotes. The Moneydarragh locals also told me there was a good chance that the summer sun might appear in June and possibly dry the surface of the moor a little.

John and I tried to put on a pretence of calm by arranging other local aviation stories for the series, but he too was feeling the pressure. When he went filming in Italy in mid May with the series presenter Dan Snow, he left me about half a dozen different ways of contacting him, just in case I heard word from Dublin. My wife noticed I was beginning to pace around the house like a potential first time father.

As the end of May approached, my nerves were at breaking point. The archaeological authorities in Dublin had now reached the end of their indicated determining period for our application. There were diggers to book, flights to arrange and presenter Dan Snow's existing filming commitments to work around. With no word from Dublin, I couldn't arrange anything with any certainty – my time was running out. It was time to grab the archaeological bull by the horns. I rang our archaeologist Ciara, who had submitted my licence applications, to see if she had heard anything. She had left voice messages with the relevant staff but had heard nothing back. Just to add to the stress levels, Ciara explained we needed to use the official excavation licence number we were waiting for to apply for our Licence to Export. Without the former, we couldn't get the latter. To add further stress, I was informed an export licence would only be granted when a specific list of recovered items had been sent to the Irish archaeological authorities i.e. in the days or possibly weeks after the dig! The authorities indicated it was not normal procedure to get one in advance. There was a distinct possibility that we could be allowed to dig the site but then not be able to drive the items on the day over the border to Northern Ireland to start the immediate preservation these sensitive items would require. I felt despair and frustration welling up inside of me.

The export licence problem posed significant problems for the project. The team, who came from all over the UK and Europe, couldn't afford to come over for the dig, then go away again and then come back when the items were exported into Northern Ireland to assist with the cleaning.

John and I decided the best way to deal with our export licence problem was to just ignore it and concentrate instead on getting the dig licence. I note one email from this exchange is signed off *weary but not broken yet!* By now it was approaching the end of May. To cause further anxiety, some unpronounceable volcano in Iceland erupted and stopped UK and European air travel, potentially for weeks. I started to sit in corners rocking.

Finally after weeks of silence the authorities issued a Licence to Excavate, via Ciara our archaeologist, in the last week of May. When she rang me to break the joyous news, I felt too emotionally rung-out to celebrate. Without this Licence to Export, the dig was literally going nowhere and I was unable to confirm anything with those involved. This was truly bittersweet news. There were approximately 5 weeks to go to the start of our indicated dig date range.

John and I convened another one of our, by now hourly, email exchanges. I set out a reasoned debate as to why an export licence needed to be granted now for us to be permitted to remove P8074 over the border on the day. John agreed to discuss the issue with Eamonn Kelly, the Keeper of Irish Antiquities at the National Museum, to see if we could resolve this issue. I reiterated to John the reasons I had already stated in my application for seeking an export licence to be granted before the dig day. The thrust of my argument was that, once excavated, the retrieved items would need immediate cleaning and preservation at a secure location. They would begin to immediately deteriorate or be at risk of disappearing altogether if we had to leave them on the mountain side while we waited, potentially several weeks, for an export licence to be issued. I did not have the time or the money to rent a secure storage facility in Donegal and travel from my home to it to undertake the immediate preservation of this aircraft.

Producer John sent his email first thing on the last day of May. A few hours later Eamonn Kelly responded back. John's immediate email response to me continues to be one of my highlights of the entire project. Sadly it will not feature in the programme. No-one watching the Bud Wolfe episode will ever know how much work went into the licencing of this project or how agonisingly stressed John and I had become during these last few weeks. In this single 3 line email, John Hayes Fisher distilled the very essence of the tortuous journey we had travelled together. This was the moment when I could finally breathe out, slump to the floor and say without fear of contradiction that I was now officially permitted to attempt to retrieve P8074. This was my champagne popping moment!

His email in its full glory read:
"I think we might have just got it!
Can you translate as it's all archaeological speak to me ??? !!!
I'm finding it difficult to contain myself!"

Eamonn had responded positively, removing any of the delay issues that surrounded the export licence. It was to be issued shortly and certainly before the day of the dig! However, Eamonn felt it was a good time to announce that I would now require a fourth licence that we had never heard of before – a Licence to Alter! Technically, under the archaeological legislation we were 'altering' an excavated archaeological object i.e. the recovered aircraft metal, by proposing to wash it and apply protective varnishes. However Ned said there was no urgency in applying for this licence.

To obtain the Licence to Export, the authorities were happy for us to submit to them in advance of the dig, a likely list of items to be retrieved based on our experience from previous Spitfire digs. Once preservation was complete, we could finalise this with them and provide a definitive list of items exported. A great result and Ned's best wishes for the success of the project were a great boost at a time when my energy levels were at an all time low.

This good news enabled me to finalise all the loose ends with the rest of the team. Taking into account everyone's availability, we chose 28th June as dig day. Flights were booked, leave was requested from employers and Dan the presenter confirmed his availability. I finalised our last minute requirements with Danny Kearney who had been chosen to carry out the excavation. We were going to be working with two diggers on the day and I decided to upgrade the smaller one to a 14 ton version. This was just in case the big long reach got stuck. It would also be useful for moving the excavated remains from the crash site to the nearby roadside for collection and transportation back to Derry. I also ensured we had all the protective fencing and signs we would need to cordon off the dig site.

Danny took our growing list in his stride and quickly got to work procuring all we needed. Anything additional we sought from him was always met with a comforting 'No problem' He was very excited about undertaking the dig in the area where he was brought up. To prevent the risk of the story getting out into the press at this stage and any attempts by individuals at an illegal excavation at the site, all involved were sworn to secrecy about the exact crash location and the dig date. Poor Danny frequently had to deny all knowledge of any involvement when questioned. He chuckled uncomfortably, saying this was usually on the way in or out of Mass. I typed him a brief document giving him all the dates and times of when he had to be ready on the moor and the equipment we needed. It also contained some background information on the crash and the pilot Bud Wolfe. "When I have read this, he joked, waving the papers at me "do you want me to burn it?"

Derry City Council who had supported the project from its early days, set about delivering all the materials and equipment I would require in the immediate days after the excavation. This included engine oil, polyurethane varnish, brushes, protective gloves and a small pallet truck for moving the Merlin engine around during cleaning.

Now that it was officially going ahead, a few last minute emails were required. I notified the Estate Manager for Lord Shaftesbury in Dorset to let him know we had finally been given official approval to dig. Bud's daughters Betty and Barbara were also given the good news. We had talked about this between us for so many months and now it was going to happen. While excited their father's aircraft could potentially soon be excavated, they were naturally concerned that their father's story could soon become global news. This was completely understandable. There were a few inaccurate stories about Bud and his time in the Curragh. Many, the daughters felt, he would have found offensive. I promise them that we would only use 100% historical documented fact.

Soon it was the start of June and it was with much relief that I headed off to Barcelona with my sadly neglected wife for a few days of culture. I didn't want to see or hear anything at all about Spitfires or diggers for the next three days. Producer John said he was joking when he asked me to keep my phone handy, although I wasn't so sure. He asked the day before I left whether all was in order.

"Just a few small things to arrange when I get back" I replied calmly. "A media strategy and the small issue of legally possessing 6 Browning machine guns and 750 rounds of ammunition"

And given what I had achieved in the last few months, John agreed these small issues could wait until I got back.

CHAPTER 8

The Small Matter of Several Machine Guns

So far, the whole project had deliberately been kept hush-hush. Only half a dozen people knew the precise location of the crash site on the moor. Under the archaeological legislation there was an onus on the team to keep the site secret to prevent any illegal tampering. Now with less than a month to go, it still wasn't time to let the cat completely out of the bag, but I could start to untie the knot and let kitty wave a leg around enticingly.

I compiled a list of the key newspapers and radio stations in the North and South of Ireland and typed up press articles that outlined what was to be attempted the following month. They were kept deliberately vague, just a few details on the crash and the aircraft. I did not wish to disclose Bud's name at this point. As the day of the dig got closer, I intended to increase the supply of details of the event to the press. I was very aware that I didn't want the world and his cousin to turn up on the day and be in close proximity to a potentially dangerous hole and two large diggers.

The other factor I had to consider was that the event was to be filmed by the BBC for broadcasting at a much later date. Accordingly I went for just radio and paper coverage and hoped that the other television channels wouldn't turn up. I assumed other channels wouldn't want to give major air time to a forthcoming BBC series. At the end of the day, 360 Production were filming my excavation. They were my guests and the potential media coverage was none of their making. They could help where they could but effectively, I had to be my own one man media department for the project. Press releases had to be prepared to give out on the day of the dig and I also had to input into the BBC web site news article that would publicise the event from 6am on the day of the dig.

The honour of breaking the news went to the Irish News – a daily paper printed in Belfast that covers Northern Ireland and Co Donegal. They had been a good supporter of the original project to find the City of Derry Airport Spitfire. Now I went back to them with the news of a definite excavation attempt at another site. Understandably I had to be vague in the details and their reporter understood this. He was happy to be getting the scoop on our proposed dig. In fact something about Spitfires or just digging large holes seemed to appeal to every journalist to whom I spoke.

On the 6th June, the Irish News ran a full page story on the proposed dig referring discretely to Spitfires, the Inishowen Peninsula, brief details on the pilot's family and the risk of putting big diggers into a bog. The amusing thing about this article was that the interview was done the day before I left for a short break in Barcelona. My wife and I were looking forward to hopefully 72 Spitfire free hours. Whilst in Barcelona, their reporter rang me to proof read the article over the phone. My wife and I were enjoying a very nice meal, 'wine had been taken' and I remember waking up the next day and telling her I had very little recollection of what I had talked about. Therefore it was with a little apprehension that I bought a copy of the paper at Belfast International Airport when we returned to see what I had said. A quick scan thankfully revealed nothing libellous or slanderous.

Our proposed attempt at the first fully licensed excavation of a WW2 aircraft in Ireland soon captured the imagination of the press on both sides of the border. Papers the length and breadth of the country began contacting the BBC for further details who in turn directed them to 360 Production in Derry who passed them onto me. My poor mobile phone didn't know what hit it. In successive articles, I revealed more details; Bud's name, the licencing procedure and the extreme risk at attempting such a recovery on a deep bog. Some papers began to publish several articles a week. Radio interviews were booked in and done as everyone scrambled for new facts. Obviously feeling left out, several major daily papers from England made up what they wanted and published it under 'exclusive' banners, complete with photographs of unknown people standing on the moor claiming to be part of the team. Meanwhile the banter on the aviation websites and related chat room forums was escalating into a frenzy.

It was all so beautifully surreal as I tried to fit this in around my day job. Like a true spin doctor, I decreed I could only do radio interviews during my lunch hour. Newspaper interviews had to wait until I got home. In hindsight, it was really no fun being a one person media department. I asked my 6 year old daughter Grace would she be my PR person, but her salary demands were too excessive. Fame had sadly gone to her head since finding the Spitfire. She spent most of her time telling producer John that the programme should be called 'Grace's Spitfire' whenever he visited our house. I had to soldier on alone.

The last thing I had to do a few days before the event was finally let the cat out of the bag. After months of secrecy, my heart was pounding as I rang the reporters to tell them exactly what was happening and where. The journalists were given the date, time, location of the dig and the full extent of what we were proposing. Given the uniqueness of our proposed undertaking, they hastily rearranged their diaries to ensure they could attend.

I also advised them that from a photographic point of view there was likely to be a discrete military presence on the moor on the day and I would appreciate if they would keep their lenses on the dig and not pointed at the soldiers. Naturally curious they all asked why. I let them know there was the distinct possibility of the dig uncovering 6 Browning .303 machine guns and approximately 1000 rounds of ammunition which had not been recovered a the time of the crash. Soldiers in 1941 recovered possibly two of the weapons and significant quantities of ammunition the day after the crash. I also added that this Spitfire and these particular weapons had claimed one German bomber, a JU88 as a 'probable', while being flown by a different squadron and pilot, a few months before crashing. One curious journalist saw through the excitement and asked "How on earth do you get permission to dig up and take machine guns from Donegal to Derry?"

A reasonable question given Northern Ireland's previously troubled past. However to be honest, although it had the potential to be the most contentious part of the project to arrange, I found it to be by far the most easily arranged. From start to finish it took 10 days. The respective authorities in Northern Ireland and the Republic of Ireland were quite simply magnificent.

The Police Service of Northern Ireland (PSNI) - Firearms and Explosive Branch, the Northern Ireland Office (NIO) - Protective Security Unit and the Irish Department of Defence had been generally kept in the loop as to my progress in licencing the project. Until I had the official go ahead, I wasn't really in any position to engage fully with them and make concrete arrangements. Now that it was all systems go, these three organisations effortlessly shifted up several gears and examined possible scenarios by which these weapons could be legally excavated, possessed and eventually displayed in Northern Ireland.

Emails fired back and forth over the legislative requirements and key issues – "Would the weapons have to be decommissioned?" "What would a decommissioned machine gun look like?"; and "Would it be right to decommission such historical archaeological objects?".

In terms of Northern Ireland (NI) firearm legislation, it was proposed that if the dig recovered the weapons, then they would eventually be displayed in Derry along with the rest of the restored aircraft. This required Derry City Council Museum Services to legally possess them on their Museum general firearms licence. This licence covers them for all their antique weapons and cannons etc that they display in their museums. Permission to possess such weapons is granted by the NIO in consultation with the PSNI. They quickly liaised and it was agreed that decommissioning such historic weapons, if they were recovered, would be a brutal and historically insensitive act and would destroy the display value of the weapons. In an enlightened piece of thinking they agreed the weapons would be licenced as prohibited weapons and would therefore be left in the same condition as they were found. There would be no requirement for each weapon to have its breech block partially cut through or the barrel to be sealed in a manner that decommissioning usually requires. For security purposes the firing blocks and other removable innards would be removed and stored separately in NI. From a display viewpoint, no-one would ever notice. The NIO officials duly amended the Council licence to cover these weapons and on the day they required me to ring them immediately with the serial numbers of each recovered weapon.

With the relevant firearm authorities in NI happy, this just left me with small matter of obtaining permission from the Irish Department of Defence to cover the legal and safe excavation and possession of the weapons on the day while we were in Co Donegal. The primary responsibility for the maintenance of law and order in the Republic of Ireland rests with the Garda Siochana. The Defence Forces, pursuant to their role in rendering aid to the civil power, assist the Gardai as required. The Gardai in Moville were extremely helpful in assisting in this part of the project. They were naturally very interested in what I was proposing and were quick to offer help in liaising with the Defence Forces and to provide a police presence on the day and crowd / traffic control if needed. Sgt Lynch from Moville met me on several occasions up at the moor, to discuss progress and confirm arrangements for the Brownings. He was excellent in this regard and a first class ambassador for the Gardai, particularly as what we were proposing was unique and had no precedent on which he could rely.

But it was the actions of the Press and Information Officer at the Department of Defence, a lady by the name of Aine Fitzpatrick, who encapsulated in her efforts, the typical positive response I got from people when I rang seeking help or advice. It was now less than three weeks to dig day and I had yet to arrange anything in relation to having the relevant Irish authorities attend to oversee the excavation of the weapons. At this stage, I needed the Civil Servant equivalent of a bull in a china shop, someone who could cut through the potential red tape I could see looming and deliver a positive result quickly. Aine was that one person army. I emailed her out of the blue at the end of the first week in June. In an email, in which I recall every second word was 'urgent' I enquired what was the procedure in Ireland for assisting civilians to legally recover war time machine guns from crash sites and take them to Northern Ireland.

Now most people would have treated this as a crank call, but I got an almost immediate response, acknowledging this was a rather unique request, possibly without any current existing protocols and she would get back to me.

Two days later a representative from the Irish Defence Force Ordnance team got in touch. Aine had given them an initial briefing and they would be responsible for overseeing the recovery and were actually very keen to assist. Two days after that, Aine was back seeking a list of all the officials, I had liaised with in relation to archaeological licences, Gardai discussions and similar arrangements for holding the weapons in Derry. A week after that, she was back in touch. She had agreement from the Executive Branch within the Department of Defence and confirmation that a letter would be posted out to me stating all was in order and I could legally dig the weapons and remove the ammunition under the supervision of the Ordnance team. The next day the letter arrived to me at work and raised many curious eyebrows as it circulated around the internal mail system. From start to finish it had taken her just 10 working days. She was the epitome of enthusiasm and helpfulness.

As promised, a Captain from the 4th Western Brigade Ordnance team was immediately in contact with me to assess the scope and scale of our project and to develop a protocol as to how we would all work together on the day.

Captain Lambe envisaged a small team of technicians plus a few precautionary sentries to be present throughout the dig. Their role would be to take any weapons and bullets we found and immediately make them safe at the site. It was highly likely, I explained, that these weapons would have been routinely loaded and ready to fire on the last mission in 1941, so we were naturally concerned about the presence of live bullets in the breech.

Discussions centred around health and safety concerns and a preference for their work on the day to be kept discrete. Given the often sensitive nature of their day to day work, there was a initial indication that any filming of the Ordnance team should focus on the guns and not on the personnel undertaking this work. This was fine with me. I was delighted to have the best possible team undertaking this aspect of the project and I soon developed an excellent working relationship with the team based in Custume Barracks in Athlone.

I briefed the team on the physics of a high speed plane crash and how we proposed to excavate the port and starboard wing areas first. From experience, this would reveal very little in the way of surviving wing structure but possibly the remaining weapons from the fighter's armament.

The dynamics of the crash would mean that these weapons would have been projected lance – like through the wing structure and deep into the soft peat. The wings themselves tend to end up in the upper few feet of the crash profile or, more often than not, lying on it. The Mk IIa Spitfire carried a total of 8 Browning .303 machine guns. We knew from the historical documents, that 1, possibly 2 weapons had been recovered by the Army in 1941. That left us facing the possibility of recovering 6 or 7. If we went for the wing regions first, we should find these weapons fairly early in the dig and this would give the Ordnance team time to work on them throughout the day.

Each gun carried approximately 350 rounds of ammunition, enough for a 12-14 second burst of continuous fire. In reality pilots were taught to fire only 1-2 seconds bursts at a time. Our weapons were Mk II variants, made under licence from Browning by Birmingham Small Arms (BSA) based in Small Heath, England. They also produced other types of weapons for the war effort. The BSA version was based on a standard Browning 1919 Model design that had remained unchanged for over 20 years. To satisfy the requirements of the RAF, the design was adapted from the original Browning .300 calibre to enable it to operate the standard RAF .303 calibre bullet. The internal springs were also strengthened to allow a much faster rate of fire. BSA went into Browning production for the Air Ministry in March 1939. Initially they were producing 2,400 weapons a month. Soon however output had rocket by 800% and peaked in March 1942 at 16,400 weapons a month. A truly staggering performance. During the course of WW2, BSA produced nearly half a million Browning machine guns and spares equivalent to a further 100,000. This was despite being the target of several Luftwaffe bombing raids, particularly a series of raids in November 1940 which killed 53 and halted rifle production at the plant for 3 months.

From a war time service perspective, our weapons also possessed a significant history. On the 4th April 1941, P8074 was being flown by F/Lt E. H. Thomas as Red 1 with 222 (Natal) Squadron. It and another Mk II Spitfire (Red 2 - P/O N.H.D. Ramsay) left Coltishall at 1541 hours. At about 1640 hours, the combat report states that Red 2 sighted an enemy aircraft about 4 miles away. They were 15 miles out to sea, north east of the town of Cromer, which is on the north Norfolk coast. F/Lt Thomas in P8074 immediately closed and identified the German aircraft as a JU 88. The JU 88 was a twin engined extremely versatile high speed bomber that carried a crew of three and numerous forward and rear firing machine guns located around the cockpit. These were large calibre weapons than those equipping the RAF fighters at the time. At about 350 yards, he opened fire with a short burst and noticed that the enemy aircraft *'jinked a bit'* having apparently been taken by surprise.

As Red 1 closed to 200 yard and opened fire again, accurate return fire was experienced from the lower rear gunner in the JU 88. Two bullets penetrated the leading edge of P8074's port wing, main spar, centre ammunition tanks and finished up in the landing light. Red 1 continued to close to about 70 yards firing all the time as the JU 88 climbed towards the cloud cover at 7,000 feet. The effect of Red 1's fire was to cause both engines to smoke furiously while pieces fell of the port engine cowling. Red 2 also fired all his ammunition and saw more pieces fly off the enemy aircraft which managed to stagger in to the thick cloud and when last seen was beginning to lose height.

The JU 88 work number 4224, coded V4+AR failed to return to base. Lt E. Menge and his crew were recorded as lost by the Luftwaffe records. The RAF claimed the bomber as a 'probable' and in the action P8074 had been damaged and required minor repairs.

For display purposes at the Council Museum, I was only interested in retaining the weapons after the dig. Any recovered magazines containing belts of .303 ammunition would be retained by the Ordnance team. However I was to find that even the humblest little war time bullet has its admirers and during my Army negotiations an email arrived from an unexpected source. The Head of Communications and Heritage at BAE Munitions, England contacted me to enquire if it would be possible to get a few samples of any recovered bullets for their museum. During WW2, he explained, they had manufactured the vast majority of the Allies .303 ammunition at their Radway Green factory. They had very little in the way of 1941 ammunition and were keen to get some for their display. Another job to go on the list.

Captain Lambe and I agreed that it would be best for the Ordnance team to retain the weapons, if they were recovered, in the safety of Custume Barracks until such times as they had been fully cleaned and inspected. Several of his team expressed a desire to assist in the cleaning and the preservation of the weapons. I was more than happy for his expert team to undertake this aspect of the work. When they were ready for display I could arrange their collection in due course. To keep the process legal and above board, I drew up a simple template for the Ordnance team to use to record the serial numbers of the guns and sign that they had taken possession of all the weapons on the day.

What the Defence Forces team were proposing to do had now surpassed our original request for help. Not only would they oversee the safe recovery of the weapons and bullets, they were now going to clean and make the weapons safe ready for museum display and hold onto them until we were ready to collect them. Several crates of beer were put on the shopping list in appreciation. All our Defence Force discussions were confidential as they, like us didn't want a large public turn out to watch the potentially dangerous excavation and recovery of these possibly loaded weapons. With less than a week to go to dig day, one paper decided to publish the date, time and location of the dig. The world and his cousin had just been invited! I rang the Ordnance team to advise them of this slight hiccup. They were just reading the article in the Officers Mess their Senior Officer told me. "Not to worry" he commented "We'll just treble the armed guard – give you a secure military cordon!" Now I was undertaking an excavation in the middle of a major Army exercise. I made a note to add a lot more beer to the shopping list.

And that was it all organised! I could relax slightly and begin to enjoy it. It was going to happen. Well it would, if the diggers didn't sink on the way down to the crash site. How I had got to this stage still escapes me. My friends thought I was daft, my own father said I would never find it and my wife hoped that hopefully she might see a bit more of me in future. Some said it was fate, others said it was down to luck. Perhaps.

Seneca the Younger was a Roman philosopher and statesman. He said: *Luck is a collision between opportunity and good preparation*. He was certainly right in this case. I took a few minutes to relax one evening in the garden. As I sat there catching my breath, I recalled my happy Airfix childhood, hanging badly made Spitfires from my bedroom ceiling. Now in 48 hours time, I was to oversee the actual excavation of one of these iconic aircraft from a remote bog, in front of a potentially large crowd and a film crew. What a dream!

TE Lawrence said in his 1922 novel 'The Seven Pillars of Wisdom':
"All men dream, but not equally. Those who dream by night in the dusty recesses of their minds wake in the day to find that it was vanity; but the dreamers of the day are dangerous men, for they may act their dream with open eyes, to make it possible."

CHAPTER 9

Deep Holes and Excavations

The day before the dig was to commence, we prepared to assemble and move the heavy machinery down to the actual crash site. The entire project could still go spectacularly and disastrously wrong at this late stage. If the long reach digger became bogged down somewhere on the site, we were in serious trouble. It would be highly unlikely we could rustle up an alternative digger at such short notice. This was the frayed nerves day. This truly was make or break. The final preparation began with the arrival of the advance party of the aviation team.

The Welsh contingent, Gareth, Glyn and Philippa, took the overnight boat to Belfast and arrived at my house mid morning. We set off for the moor to meet Danny Kearney and his diggers at the site. As we came over the hill towards the site, a small cheer went up from inside the car as we saw one of the diggers already parked at the side of the moor.

Danny met us and outlined his progress so far. Firstly he apologetically broke the news that the transporter with the big digger onboard was delayed due to a flat tyre. He had also ordered several loads of hardcore to firm up the existing track that ran for a distance from the road into the moor. It was vital that this provided a firm surface for all those essential cars and lorries that had to be close to the site – the TV people, the Gardai and the EOD team. In its previous boggy state, Danny quite rightly considered, it would have become unusable after 10 minutes with the passage of heavy vehicles. With a few loads of stone and 30 minutes scooping about with the digger, he created a quality track that would serve us well over the days ahead and the local Moneydarragh peat cutters for many years to come.

The bog mats had also arrived. Essentially these are very large wooden railway sleepers, about 6 meters long and a meter wide, cabled together in pairs to form large mats. These are then used by the diggers to sit on and spread their weight over a greater surface area to reduce the risk of the digger sinking into the bog. These were important pieces of equipment, very expensive to hire, but completely essential. We had 18 sets to ensure we got from the road to the crash site - about 500 meters. Some parts of the route down were quite solid and wouldn't require the use of mats. Others sections were completely waterlogged and it was for traversing these that the mats would earn their keep.

While we waited for the long reach digger to arrive we got busy marking out the site with safety fencing. We set up a large perimeter around the crash point and the area where the diggers would be operating. We fenced off another area which the Army EOD team could use to work on the weapons. Finally we marked out an area where the public could safely sit on the rising ground over the site and watch the proceedings. All this was done in glorious sunshine. We soon had all the Health and Safety signs in place and the vegetation around the crater trimmed back to reveal the gentle depression the crash had created.

Mid afternoon, Danny shouted to us that the transporter would be here in a few minutes. We all assembled at the roadside eagerly straining our eyes for the first glimpse of this large digger. When it came into view, I think we all thought the same thing instantaneously: "How is that thing going to get over the bog without disappearing down into its depths?" To me, a non-digger expert, it was a beast, 24 tons with an arm that seemed to go on forever. While we all exchanged slightly worried glances, Danny's team of Michael, Kevin and Paddy soon had this leviathan off the lorry and parked beside the other smaller digger ready to begin the slow trek down to the crater.

In terms of watching skilled men at work and making it look easy, what happened next was a text book demonstration. Working in tandem, like two orange dinosaurs running a relay race, the diggers confidently moved forward, collecting a mat and tenderly placing it in the path of the advancing digger. It in turn drove on to this mat, collected one from behind and placed it again in front of the other. And so they proceeded down the slope, occasionally slipping and quickly steadying themselves. Finally after nearly two hours they arrived at the crater. Michael, who was driving the big digger, made a nest of bog mats, wiggled his digger around on top of them to bed them down and declared he was happy and switched the machine off. It had been a privilege to watch this display. It took a few seconds for it to sink in that we had actually got the diggers in place. I could see it but I couldn't quite believe it.

Befitting such a monumental event, I texted producer John accordingly. The message simply said: "The Eagle has landed! You are good to go tomorrow".

With the diggers in place, 4 happy aviation archaeologists congratulated Danny and his team again and returned to the hotel in Derry where the rest of the aviation dig team, Steve, Vickie, Jeff and Simon and the 360 crew had now assembled. It was time for a beer, food and some happy banter.

Dig day started early. It was breakfast at 6 45am which completely defeats the enjoyment of staying in a hotel. John was already in the dining room monitoring the BBC story which had just been released on their web site. Interest had already started to develop. Dan intended to update his many followers via Twitter throughout the day and the 360 staff were also going to keep the company Facebook site well stocked with progress and pictures. Far from being a discrete dig in a remote part of the Inishowen peninsula, technology was going to permit people around the world to follow events as they happened. This was great news as it allowed Betty and Barbara and the extended Wolfe family across the USA to cheer us on.

A convoy of cars left Derry at 7 30am and headed for the site. To get us in the mood, a CD of classic WW2 war film themes was blaring out of the car stereo. We swung round the last bend, to the strains of the Dambusters March, just in time to see the Irish Defence Force Ordnance team arriving. I remember unprintable Welsh exclamations of surprise emanating from the back seat as a sea of camouflage spread out of the trucks and jeeps and disappeared around the site. Such digs don't usually require such a large Army presence but it certainly looked very impressive as they established perimeters and inner cordons. It was like the film set for Saving Private Ryan, only slightly smaller.

At about 8 30am, John briefed us on what he wanted to film and the various pieces to camera he needed before we started digging. From past experience we knew that we wouldn't be digging anytime soon, so those that weren't needed immediately to say something to the camera made a mad rush to the catering stand to top up with coffee while the sound man chased after us trying to pin radio mikes to those that needed them. While these pieces were being filmed, I had a chance to look around the site and noticed that it was slowly but surely starting to fill up with people. All over the site, things were happening – it was a hive of activity. No doubt about it, there was quite a carnival atmosphere building and even better, the sun was still shining.

Garda Lynch strolled across the site with a broad smile to reassure me that he and 30 armed soldiers had everything under control. The Radio Foyle outside broadcast car had just arrived and was being set up by their reporter. If someone had told me there was a stall at the side of the road selling Gleneely Spitfire souvenir T-shirts I wouldn't have been surprised. Captain Lambe indicated he was happy with the location we had prepared for his team and they were all set up and ready for us. It was agreed that each gun, if and when it was excavated, would be handed over by me to him, the serial number recorded on a sheet and then I would ring these numbers through to the various firearm officials that needed them.

The press had arrived in strength and all looked suitably shocked at the scale of our proposed project on this large open site. Finally the Queens University Team arrived, bringing Ciara our professional archaeologist. They brought a fantastic mix of James Bond type kit that they intended to wave around the excavated hole to survey it in 3D and plot the position of the key items of wreckage. Later back in their lab, they intended to produce a virtual scan of the crater with the depth and position of these bits. From this, they could speculate the dynamics of the impact – speed, inclination etc which would be useful when we produced our archaeological write up of the excavation.

To complete the aviation team complement, our last team member Baz arrived at the crater. He had just driven for 36 hours from Holland to be here. "Sorry I'm late" he said before staggering off to the catering stand for a dangerously large coffee injection.

The interested locals of Moneydarragh arrived to claim the best seats. There were deck chairs and wind breaks getting erected around the upper slopes. One local woman joked to me that this was the biggest thing to hit Moneydarragh since the plane in '41. I even met a Japanese family who were holidaying in Ireland and had travelled to Co Donegal specifically to watch the excavation attempt. The journalists soon got themselves organised and started asking me for a few minutes of my time for a quote or a picture. I took a few minutes to give them the latest and explained that the team would endeavour to give them as many picture opportunities as we could, but to please work with us on what was clearly going to be a busy day. The press conveniently congregated into one corner which made it easier for me to update them.

John was eventually satisfied that he had all his pieces to camera. Gareth and Steve had been filmed jumping up and down on the springy crater surface and poking at its innards with long thin metal poles. Dan had strode back and forth across the moor, like a Bronte character, explaining to the cameras why we were here and what we hoped to achieve. And for the millionth time - or so it felt – I explained to Dan all I knew about Bud and this crash and how Grace and I had found this site.

"That'll do" said John "let's dig!" The team split off into their various roles. Some were required to stay around the crater and be available to explain to the cameras what we were finding. Others would carefully pick through each scoop the digger deposited behind the hole and look for anything interesting that we may want to film. Just after 10 30am, with the traditional thumbs-up to start the proceedings, Michael started up the long reach machine. A large puff of blue smoke belched from its rear and drifted down the mountain side and a small cheer rose from the crowd. We were off! As part of our archaeological licence agreement, we were required to gently scrape back the upper layers of the peat. Under Ciara's archaeological supervision, we used a toothless bucket for this part of the exercise to cause the least damage possible to any bits of wreckage we came across.

The first part of the excavation took place over what we assumed was the starboard wing area. The initial 20 minutes of digging in this location was cosmetic in nature to define a neat hole above the closest objects our detecting equipment was indicating at an approximate depth of 10ft. The only bit of aircraft we encountered on the way down to these objects was a thin bit of wing aluminium covering. Apart from this single piece, we did not see another fragment as we slowly dug down through the peat. The team started to get nervous! Then just beyond 10 ft down, as the bucket moved slowly through the soft peat, the bucket gently bumped into something with a reassuringly solid thump and scooped it up. The digger arm arched up into the bright Donegal morning and swung around to empty this load on to the moor surface. Almost immediately, the cry went up from the team working on the spoil heap. "Browning!"

Sprinting as best we could in the ankle deep peat, the camera crew and aviation archaeologists quickly swarmed around the bucket. We were all stunned at what greeted us. It was perfect. It was immaculate. Alarmingly, it also had a short belt of bullets hanging from it too. We all took a deep breath and the cameras rolled. Dan tried to find superlatives to describe our first find after only 20 minutes of digging. We gave the Browning a gentle wipe down. I was shocked by how pristine it looked. Cradling it like a newborn, I took it over to the press to briefly introduce it to them and then I handed it over to Captain Lambe and his team in their restricted area. He stared at it for a few seconds and commented he was not expecting it to look so good. He quickly directed his team to sort out the belt of ammunition hanging from the gun's side.

Within minutes, we were back digging and fairly quickly we came down onto two more Brownings. The Queens team got in with their kit and measured both weapons as being a few degrees of vertical. These two weapons were soon dug out by hand and added to the Ordnance team's rapidly growing arsenal. On their way to their work area, I detoured via the crowd behind the security fencing to show them one of the weapons. I was very aware that this was also a community day and I wanted to involve the local community and those who had travelled far to watch the proceedings. For a few minutes, I updated them and answered as many questions as I could, before a shout of "Where's Jonny?" emanated from producer John. "Sorry folks!" I apologised, "back to work".

The next scoop from the digger produced both magazines for these weapons. The spoil team were standing over many hundred rounds of bright shiny .303 rounds. I noticed at this stage, that far from adopting a very low profile, the Ordnance technicians were now giving a first class display to a sizeable crowd on how to field strip and make safe a Browning. Certain Dads, using the pretence 'their little sons couldn't see what was happening', pushed their youngsters and themselves to the front of the fencing to watch. 'Airfix Dads!' we all agreed.

The weapons were laid out on canvas for all to see and a few badly misshapen rounds were scattered beside them for anyone to safely photo. The remaining rounds, many of them perfect, were quickly locked away in the Ordnance team's truck. Their approach to doing this work in public was much appreciated by the onlookers and was a credit to the professionalism of the team.

As we dug down to ensure we had everything from the starboard area, two things struck the dig team. Firstly, there was not a trace of starboard wing structure to be found in the hole and secondly and more importantly, for a wet bog, there was no water gathering in our deepening hole. This was great news, but it clearly baffled the Queens team who predicted 30ft of wet peat and led to some good natured exchanges at the expense of the academics. In fact, at 16ft the peat disappeared completely and was replaced by fine blue clay with a consistency like toothpaste. Alastair Ruffell from Queens University had indicated during our March survey that we were likely to be working in at least 30 ft of wet peat. On seeing the peat disappear and this clay appear, he joked his survey equipment was going into the bottom of this hole when the dig it was all over, and he stormed off in a mock huff to the catering stand which was doing great business.

We repeated the same operation on the port side of the aircraft and removed a further three Brownings. These also were in immaculate condition and were found in a vertical orientation at a depth of 16ft. This suggested to us that the port wing had struck the ground slightly before the starboard wing. The port wing with the greater velocity had speared its guns deeper into the ground. The starboard wing striking the ground a fraction after this, had slowed down enough to send its weapons only 10 ft into the ground. We were also able to deduce from the grouping of the retrieved weapons that the Irish Army in 1941 had recovered the outer Browning machine gun from each wing. We had found the inner 3 weapons from each wing. It was observations like this and the inclination of the weapons that would make our subsequent archaeological report come alive by detailing the physics of a high speed air crash. Likewise, we also found no trace of the port wing structure, which suggested both wings had been sheared off by the impact and left on the surface in 1941.

Lunch was called and while the others went for a sandwich, I caught up with the journalists to update them. My phone had also been ringing away throughout the morning. I cleared all my voice messages and missed calls before the dig started. By 12 30pm I had received a total of 86 calls, missed calls, messages and texts – all Spitfire related! Each time I tried to answer it, I had to dig through layers of waterproof clothing before trying to slide it open with my peat covered hands. It soon was looking very sorry for itself. Fearing for its life expectancy, I handed it to a friend and appointed him as my official PA for the day. Dan and the team were tweeting away and soon the viewing figures were coming back from the BBC website people.

"Second most popular story of the day and rising" was producer John's happy cry. The global appeal of this seemed endless. There were supportive emails from Canada and America congratulating us and willing us on. It was all so gloriously surreal. I have frequently used the word 'surreal' in describing this project to people and the events contained in this book. Surreal is the only way to describe it. As we dug, the whole world appeared to be looking over our shoulder.

Lunch was over, and everyone was refuelled and ready to go. Apart from me! I had spent the last 30 minutes talking to the press and the crowd and was just going for a sandwich, if there were any left, when the "Where's Jonny?" cry went up. "I need you now for a progress piece to camera" insisted John. "I need food" I pleaded. We haggled and eventually agreed that I could hold a sandwich as I was doing my piece. John was all heart!

Digging began again in earnest. We were going to follow the impact point for the fuselage down into the depths of the clay. For the next half hour we dug and enlarged the hole. There was still no sign of water which was a blessing, but worryingly, there was no sign of any fuselage wreckage either.

As we searched for the fuselage, my wife and family arrived. Andree had received permission to take Dylan and Grace out of school early to watch 'what their father was up to'. As she walked across the moor and saw the site for the first time, she finally understood what all the fuss was about and the scale of what I had been organising.

At about 25ft down, there was a loud crunching noise. Immediately, Michael pulled the digger arm back and gently scraped away the surrounding clay. The tell-tale scent of aviation fuel rose up into the air. We had now come down on the very rear end of the aircraft fuselage. We had uncovered the tail. With the skill of a surgeon, Michael deftly scraped left and right and exposed the crumpled column of shiny aluminium. We looked carefully. We could see red fabric – the proud remnants of the Irish linen that once covered the tail rudder of this aircraft. The state of preservation was incredible and caught us all by surprise. We knew it had the potential to be good but this was top drawer stuff. Even John was smiling. In fact he slapped me on the back and said that he was now prepared to believe the plane was there after all.

We studied the crumpled remains for about 10 minutes as we deliberated on how best to proceed. What we were looking at was the fuselage of the aircraft which had been vertically compacted into a crumpled mass about 6 ft long. The fuselage of a Spitfire, from the tip of its nose to its tail is a fraction under 30ft. P8074, in a ¼ of a second, had struck the bog at 350mph and compacted itself to an unrecognisable fraction of its former length. The tail was exposed on top of the wreckage column and beneath it, a few more metres down, lay the cockpit area. Somewhere underneath all of that lay the Rolls Royce Merlin engine. A buzz went through the crowd who were now also catching the strong stench of aviation fuel. Raising the guns had been exciting, but this phase of the dig was likely to be even better. This was going to lead us down to the cockpit in which Bud had flown. It was quite poignant. The last person to touch some of these cockpit controls had been Bud. Potentially in a few moments time human hands would respectfully hold them again 70 years later.

Having discussed and agreed our approach, the digger carefully lifted the first scoop of fuselage out. The sound of tearing metal was agonising, it felt like we were hurting the aircraft, but we had no alternative. The hole was 25ft deep. We couldn't risk putting anyone down there to carefully snip away control wires than ran through the crumpled remains like arteries and veins.

To cheers, the first scoop was hoisted clear into the sky and swung over to the spoil team. It was a mass of metal. They quickly swung into action shouting out the names of identifiable bits, while John directed his cameras onto key pieces. We all marvelled at the state of preservation. The tail rudder, despite being broken internally in three pieces, was virtually intact wrapped mummy like in its original linen covering. Jeff pulled out the tail wheel – still inflated, still swivelling and still proudly showing the Dunlop makers name on the tyre. The tail wheel was held up for the press corner and the overcast afternoon was lit up by the flashes of numerous cameras. Large sections of fuselage were also retrieved, still bearing the original camouflage paint. The tail fin was washed down and it still defiantly showed a portion of the RAF red, white and blue tail stripe.

Ciara weaved in and out of the wreckage pointing at significant areas of exposed paintwork. These needed to be covered in wet peat or newspaper straight away to avoid them drying and crumbling away in front of our eyes. She ensured that the excavation was undertaken in a professional archaeological manner as agreed with the authorities in Dublin.

The next scoop brought up the section of fuselage that stretches back from immediately behind the cockpit. Many of the key pieces from this area were instantly recognisable in the bucket. The pilot's oxygen bottle, the two compressed air cylinders that powered the guns and large sections of crumpled fuselage complete with the squadron code markings still clearly visible. It was all there, it was truly Christmas come early! We stopped for a quick tea break and to clear the site around the crater. All the wreckage was loaded into large sacks and placed in a secure area under the watchful eye of the Gardai. I managed to sneak away from John and update the press. They had all been patiently waiting for the latest news. I remember panting and wheezing my way through an interview for the Mark Patterson programme on BBC NI Radio Foyle. The adrenalin was flowing, walking through the peat and mud was sapping the energy levels and I was rapidly running out of superlatives. I just about managed to convey to the listeners on Radio Foyle that we were participating in a very significant event and it was probably going to get even better. It very quickly did.

As soon as we restarted, Gareth removed a sheet of curved aluminium, slightly thicker than the usual fuselage grade, from the digger bucket. Glyn pointed at the back of it and commented that he could see writing. Gareth flicked it over. Jaws dropped! Garfield Weston's name was clearly staring at us in two inch sea grey coloured stencilled letters. We had just found the Holy Grail of pieces. We had not even dared to dream that we could find this piece. But there it was in front of us. More photographs, more excited interviews on Radio Foyle and more searching for superlatives as John set up another piece to camera. Ciara immediately packed the lettering with wet peat to prevent it from deteriorating in the fresh air and we carefully moved it to the special bag set aside for sensitive finds.

To calm down from this high, we huddled together for another team brief. Our next scoop was likely to reveal the cockpit area and with it all the dials and controls associated with this iconic fighter. Careful scrutiny of the bucket and a clean work area were essential. Down went the bucket and up came all our Christmases at once! Michael the digger driver reverently spread the contents across a portion of the moor we had set aside for this part of the dig. The team descended on the emptied spoil to pick through the instantly identifiable bits. Armour plate, the pilot's seat frame including his cushioned head rest, the radio and the cockpit door and these were only the first bits that we saw.

It was during these next 20 minutes of scrutinizing that the finds got better and better, before becoming stunning and then, moments later, unimaginable. The cockpit controls were the first to be untangled, followed by nearly all the cockpit dials. The rudder pedals, both proudly engraved with the manufacturer's name 'Supermarine', the undercarriage selector and the spade grip with the gun button. The press crowd temporarily disappeared behind a frenzy of flashing cameras. The BBC NI news team arrived seeking a short interview and it was while doing this interview that I remember seeing out of the corner of my eye, Steve lift something black and crumpled from inside the tangled cockpit controls. He held it up in front of Dan and said "That, unless I am very much mistaken, is the pilot's helmet!" The press went wild, and John's smile broadened – he was getting all this on camera, second by second, as it happened. After it was gently washed with water, Steve interrupted my interview with the BBC news team and asked me what Bud's initials were. "RLW" I replied. "Yes, definitely the right plane" he joked "that's what it says here under the ear flap". The helmet had been found wrapped around the gun sight were Bud had placed it when he knew he was baling out. Another look around also revealed his oxygen mask.

He handed the helmet to Dan, who triumphantly held it up to the camera crew and the press. It is probably the defining photograph of the dig, possibly the series. The flashes from the press corner cameras lit up the site and continued to do so for the next 5 minutes as treasure after treasure was unearthed from the cockpit region. The first aid satchel complete with all its contents, the pilot's Sutton harness that kept Bud restrained in his seat and then from deep within the honeycomb of metal, the soggy, fuel soaked, remains of the Form 700 maintenance book which the RAF used to record the daily servicing of their aircraft. Ciara was straight onto these and the other sensitive items we had just retrieved. They were labelled, gently washed and sealed in plastic bags to prevent any deterioration until such times as specialist preservation could begin. As this was happening, my phone went berserk again. Several journalists from the daily papers had returned to their offices to begin filing their stories and were missing these latest finds. The photographers at the site were ringing them to let them know about what they were missing and these journalists were now ringing me for the latest update to ensure their articles would fully capture what we were finding. A very lively period and it was a great relief when John shouted 'Break for tea!'

After a quick cup and a tidy up around the site, we focussed on the last remaining object to find. By now it was approaching 5 pm and the crowd had reduced to about 60 or 70 hardy souls who were braving the occasional squally shower. Some had been there all day and many said they weren't leaving until the engine had been found. Determined not to let them down, we returned to action. The digger worked its way vertically down through the bluish clay, beyond where we had retrieved the cockpit debris. There was nothing to guide us down apart from a very dark oily stain in the clay and the reek of aviation fuel that was getting more and more noxious with every scoop. At about 30ft down, there was a metallic thump as the bucket knocked against something solid. You could feel the vibration through the peat. What ever it had struck was substantial. We peered down into the depths of the hole and there in the shadows, we could just see the back end of the Merlin engine.

It was lying there entombed in a black mass of oil and fuel soaked clay. Sitting just above it, was the propeller hub complete with the partial remains of the 3 wooden blades. The hub had been torn off in the crash as the wooden blades, rotating at 50 times per second, had slashed into the peat and instantly smashed themselves into splintered fragments. Only short sections of wood projected from the heavy metal hub which had been wrenched from the front of the engine and thrust back to its rear by the impact. Once this item was safely retrieved, the long reach digger carefully nibbled away at the surrounding mud to leave the engine sitting exposed. The engine was not quite vertical. We are all delighted to see that from a distance it looked remarkably intact. With a deft touch of the controls, Michael gently coaxed the 650 kg engine into his bucket and began to slowly lift it. The press corner and the crowd readied themselves. The Merlin was airborne again! To cheers and applause, this incredible piece of aviation engineering rose from the depths and soared momentarily across a short stretch of the Donegal sky before being gently lowered to the ground.

Fuel was pouring out of it and the call quickly went up to the crowd, who were advancing to gaze at the Merlin, to stop smoking and move back. We carefully removed some of the excess mud and with the aid of lifting straps the small digger turned it the right way up. All you could do was stare at it. It was beautiful. It had a few dents in the front. Apart from that, it was perfect!

The team and I were delighted at the success of the day. It was hard to put into words what we were all feeling. All the good descriptive words had already been used up by lunchtime. We had essentially retrieved the entire Spitfire, apart from the wings and the main landing wheels which had been torn off and presumably recovered at the time of the crash in November 1941.

The next couple of hours were spent towing the bags of wreckage up to the roadside. Paddy and Kevin working the smaller digger undertook this part of the clean up. Michael had a final search around the bottom of the hole with the digger bucket to make sure there was nothing left. Before filling it in, he pointed out an interesting feature we had missed in our excitement. 33ft down, at the bottom of the hole, was an original small patch of moor vegetation that had been thrust down into the depths of the moor by P8074 as it tore through the peat. About 3ft square, it was stained brown, but was otherwise perfectly preserved.

With the hole soon filled and dusk rapidly descending, it was an elated dig team who gathered at the side of the road. Danny and his team would be back tomorrow to reinstate the site vegetation and fence off the hole. We on the other hand, still had to get all the remains back to my home at Claudy and securely locked away. R Robinson and Son, a sand and gravel company from my home village of Claudy, had kindly provided one of their large trucks with a hydraulic grabber on the back. It quickly loaded all the wreckage, including the prized engine, and set a course for Claudy. John, Dan and the rest of the production team had long since departed for the hotel for celebratory meals and drinks. There was a rumour of steak dinners and champagne courtesy of John when we got back to the hotel. However it soon became apparent, that by the time we delivered the wreckage to Claudy and got it locked away, it was going to be way past feeding time at the hotel.

So in the end how did this impressive band of aviation archaeologists celebrate undertaking Ireland's most successful aircraft excavation? With fish and chips in Claudy! The lorry was parked in the village car park, spreading its aviation odours for all to smell. Around it, a filthy bunch of characters equally noxious, shovelled fish and burgers and the finest fizzy drinks money could buy down their throats. To be honest, the food tasted even better than steak and champagne. As we stood there under a street light, eating food out of a bag, I think it was Jeff who joked: "That's television for you, one minute they want you and the next minute you're a nobody!"

Satisfied the Spitfire was secure at my home and having asked my wife to sleep in the garage overnight to guard the engine, we drove back to Derry to celebrate at the hotel. After one or two drinks at most, we all crawled off to our respective rooms. Most to lie in our baths in an attempt to remove mud, peat and the clinging smell of aviation fuel. Sleep came easy and next morning, in varying states of physical disrepair, we came down for breakfast. John and Dan were already there, looking refreshed and staring at their various phone gadgets and tablets. With a delighted looking face, John looked up at me: "Jonny, you might want to take the guys to the nearest paper shop after breakfast, our story has exploded – everywhere!"

CHAPTER 10

"I'm Going Out to the Garage, I May Be Some Time..."

A mass departure to the local newsagents ensued after a lively breakfast. 8 of us surrounded the newspaper stand, skimming the headlines looking for anything plane related before tucking a growing pile of papers under our arms. My P8074 scrapbook was well and truly started. We graced several front covers and beamed from countless photographs.

Back at the hotel as we said our goodbyes to the 360 staff, camera crew and Dan, John announced our story had received just under 600,000 hits and had been the second most popular story on the BBC website on the day. Not bad coverage for a small team of aviation enthusiasts, two diggers and one deep hole. John was officially happy, the BBC NI executives were delighted and we had well and truly kicked off the aircraft excavation element of Dig WW2 in style.

Back at my home, we opened the garage doors and breathed in the now familiar scent of aviation fuel. We quickly took stock of all the items we had recovered. Some of the team took to assembling a pile of large parts of aluminium fuselage carefully looking for any pieces that had sensitive painted lettering or RAF markings. These would be prioritised for immediate preservation. The rest of us endeavoured to arrange the rest of the wreckage in some form of logical order – engine, cockpit, rear fuselage and tail. Significant pieces, such as cockpit controls were grouped together for special attention. Acting on archaeological advice, Bud's helmet, flying harness, first aid kit and the Form 700 paper work were gently washed and left to soak in shallow baths of water to encourage the peat, mud and oil to loosen. In the days after, these significant items were passed to Derry City Council who had arranged for conservation specialists to assess them.

By the end of the day, the team had delivered some order out of the chaos in the garage. However, they soon had to depart for ferries and flights back to their day jobs. That left me staring at the mammoth task ahead of me. It was very easy to write in our archaeological Method Statement that I would wash and preserve the wreckage. But now, standing into my garage, staring at an almost complete Spitfire, it was an altogether different battle. Everything recovered around the cockpit region and below, including the engine and the propeller hub was cocooned in a cake of mud, oil and fuel. Every little opening was stuffed with clay. Engine oil was still oozing out of the Merlin. And with each hour, sensitive paintwork was at significant risk of crumbling away to flakes. It was time to prioritise. Paintwork items first, then the cockpit controls.

My wife stuck her head round the garage door, enquiring menacingly would it all be done by dinner time. I assured her it would, but didn't specify which dinner time. In all honesty, Christmas dinner looked the most likely!

But help was on the way. Early next morning Edwin Robinson, from Robinson's, who had transported the wreckage from Donegal, rang me to say one of their lorries was parked outside my house. He asked could I open up the garage and help their driver load up any large bits I wanted steamed and power washed. The engine, the propeller hub, radiator and armour plate were quickly hoisted aboard and spent the next 4 hours getting power washed. The cleaning transformed this 650kg lump of mud back to the instantly recognisable and iconic Rolls Royce engine. The rapid change in the Merlin's appearance gave me a considerable boost. Apart from a torn sump, everything else was intact. The cleaning of the heavy and intricate items put me weeks ahead of schedule and was typical of the way people volunteered to assist this project whenever and however they could.

For the next 5 months, most evenings, all weekends, and any time in between were spent cleaning, varnishing or spraying the recovered pieces. At the same time, to fulfil my obligations to the authorities in Dublin and the MOD, I inventoried all the pieces recovered and tagged them with reference numbers. I was also required under law to notify the MOD of any recovered personal effects of the pilot. I reported the recovery of the helmet, paperwork and first aid kit to the rather surprised MOD team and requested, if possible, that the helmet be given to the pilot's family. This was readily agreed by the MOD staff and I was able to pass this information on to Bud's daughters, Betty and Barbara, in an emotional series of phone calls in the days after the dig. They eventually decided that their father's helmet should be displayed together with the rest of the recovered items in Derry.

During these weeks, the requests for radio interviews kept coming as people sought the latest news on the preservation progress. One day, I was surprised to hear a Canadian voice on my home answering machine requesting me to participate in a radio interview for a programme called 'The Link' on the Canadian Broadcasting Corporation. When I called them back, the programme producer informed me that the success of the dig had made headlines in Canada, particularly because of the Weston connection. During the recorded interview, I informed the host that we had actually recovered the piece of the fuel tank cowling that had Garfield Weston written on it and I had just spent that afternoon carefully cleaning, drying and varnishing it. Our adventures in a bog went down really well with the programme's listeners who apparently take their war time history very seriously.

In early July, one of the Inishowen newspaper reporters rang me to say that Mr Galen Weston's personal assistant had contacted her seeking an email address for me. She let me know that Galen Weston was Garfield Weston's son. Naturally curious, I immediately got in touch and was surprised to find that indeed Galen Weston had followed the events of the dig closely and he was delighted that we had been successful in our endeavours. His assistant explained that the recovery of one of the Garfield Weston presentation Spitfires was considered as a very significant event by the Weston family. Galen Weston was keen to know what I intended to do now with P8074 and could he assist in any way. I explained the preservation was nearly complete and eventually the remains were to be displayed in one of the Derry City Council museums in the City. I joked with him that the Weston's had already paid for this Spitfire in 1940 without having to pay for it again.

However Galen Weston was not to be deterred and quietly made a sizeable donation to the Heritage and Museum Service of the Council to assist with the specialist preservation of the flying helmet and the recovered paperwork and to generally help with the long term display proposals of P8074. In my discussions with his team, I indicated that I was keen to get an appropriately worded plaque erected at the City of Derry Airport. This would fulfil Jerry Wolfe's wish, as expressed in her letter to Nat McGlinchey in 1994 to see her husband Bud remembered at the airport. It would also commemorate the Eagles, the Weston connection and, most significantly, ensure the late Nat McGlinchey's name was permanently associated with these brave fliers. They kindly agreed to fund this and I was requested to proceed with designs and suitable wording. I also let his assistant know about the radio broadcast, which had just aired in Canada a few days earlier, which I felt would fill them in on the background to the project.

I thought it fitting that the Weston stencilled piece should be offered to the Weston family. I considered this piece was very significant, both personally and historically, for Galen Weston and Canada appeared to be the logical home for its display. I suggested this to his assistant and he promised to immediately convey this offer to Mr Weston.

While all this was going on, the coverage of the excavation had been making waves of its own within the BBC. The head of 360 Production emailed the team to inform us that, while inside the BBC pitching ideas for future work, he had been flicking through the in-house BBC magazine 'Ariel'. He was surprised and delighted to find the excavation had made an article on how to reach new audiences. It was No 8 in the 10 Best Rated stories. This was tremendous for a story that had not yet had the associated programme broadcast, unlike the Top 7.

A few weeks later the Weston office got back to me. Not only was Galen Weston delighted to accept the offer of the stencilled cowling piece, but he also wanted to enquire whether my family and I would be interested in coming to Toronto at the end of September to attend the launch of a book called "Maple Leaf Empire" that he had supported. The book was written by the prominent Canadian historian and university professor Jonathan Vance. The book chronicled the development of the relationship between Canada and Great Britain between WW1 and WW2. The tie-in with the Spitfire discovery, they added was perfect, in that Jonathan Vance had included the story of Garfield Weston's purchase of the Spitfires as well as a photograph of one of the planes, with the "Garfield Weston" lettering visible on the cowling.

To demonstrate just how important the Weston's considered this stencilled piece to be, they arranged for two staff from their London office to holiday in Ireland, on the condition that they took a detour to my home in Claudy to collect it. When they arrived, they took the carefully bubble wrapped piece of cowling and placed it in a suitcase. Days after their return to London, the suitcase was then personally escorted to Canada where the piece was housed in a state of the art display case, specially commissioned by Galen Weston from The Art Gallery of Ontario. It took pride of place in the impressive reception area of the Weston's multi story office block in downtown Toronto.

This Toronto invite, as you can imagine, caused quite a sensation in the McNee household! Despite it being nearly 8 weeks away, Grace started packing that night. Recharged with this turn of events, I returned to the preservation with renewed vigour. Even Dylan and Grace got involved. Dylan in particular soon became quite an expert at picking through the quarry sacks to ensure we had not missed a significant item. In his expeditions searching around in the congealed oil and peat at the bottom of these large sacks, he unearthed an exhaust stub, some armour plated glass from the cockpit and a very deformed bullet case. Soon we had all the sacks thoroughly searched and eventually all they contained were small twisted bits of non-descript aluminium and a few lengths of cabling. These bits were not identifiable and were not suitable for museum display. Permission was granted from the Dublin authorities and the City of Derry Airport management for these 2 sacks of remnants to be buried in the future, adjacent to the now abandoned WW2 runway at the airport. It was from this runway that P8074 had flown in 1941, so it was felt by all, that this was a suitable and fitting proposal for these particular fragments that remained.

Eventually anything that could be displayed had been washed and preserved to prevent further deterioration. I now knew every rivet in the fuselage and every inch of that beautiful engine. It had not been without a price. I admit my children had become aviation orphans and my wife was truly fed up with the kitchen smelling of aviation fuel and the sink constantly being blocked with peaty sludge. "I'm just nipping out to the garage for 5 minutes" had long since ceased to be funny. I had cut myself numerous times on the sharp aluminium and with the rising price of scrap metal I was genuinely concerned for the safety of P8074 as it sat in my garage.

It was a sad day when I arranged for the Museum Department to come and take it away to a secure location. The agreement between the MOD and myself was for the remains to be put on public display in Derry. On the day they collected everything, I must admit, it was hard to see it go. I was going to miss the thrill I got every time I walked into the garage and looked at the Merlin, knowing it had once powered this aircraft after German fighters and bombers 70 years ago. The engine and everything else was packed up and taken away by the Museum staff. Soon the aroma of fuel faded from the garage and I re-introduced myself into family life again.

However the thought struck me in early August that Bud's aircraft tyres had lifted off from the runway at RAF Eglinton in November 1941 and officially never returned. This routine convoy patrol was never completed, Bud never finished his tour with his 133 squadron colleagues and P8074 never came back. I thought this was something that should be put right. We had found the rear tail wheel. It was still inflated and 100% intact. I considered it was time for it to drift over the runway one more time before touching down and rolling a few feet along the tarmac before coming to a stop. P8074 would touch down and complete her marathon mission 70 years late. I discussed the proposal with the airport management who immediately considered such a touchdown event as very symbolic. Possibly airports don't like to see their aircraft depart and never come back. I arranged the event, in conjunction with the airport and the Museum Department and invited the same journalists who had been at the dig. It was a chance for them to see the state of preservation of the tail wheel now that it was cleaned. I thought that only a few may attend as, after all it didn't rank anywhere close to the scale of the dig, but they all came and so did Derry's Mayor, Alderman Maurice Devenney. The tyre touching down again was seen as a very poignant moment in the Spitfire story and it was very well received and covered in the NI papers. The Mayor was very interested in the story and soon discussion turned to possibilities for displaying the remains in Derry. The city had recently been awarded 'UK City of Culture' status for 2013. The display of the only excavated Spitfire in Ireland would be another string to Derry's cultural bow. For the time being, that could all wait, we had suitcases to pack. We were bound for Toronto!

Toronto in late September was a pleasant change from wet and windy Claudy. Our first impression as we drove to our hotel was of a bustling city with a vibrant mix of nationalities and stunning architecture. Dylan and Grace were very excited about going to the book launch, so much so in fact that Dylan asked me to buy him his first suit. Next day, the family headed downtown in search of the Weston offices. The taxi driver left us at the foot of a grand entrance. We got out and looked around and then we looked up! The Weston Centre is an octagonal shaped, high rise building 20 storeys tall. It is the HQ for the Weston world-wide business empire. We took the elevator to the 19th floor and walked out into a very impressive double height reception area with a sweeping metal stair case that led to Galen Weston's offices on the 20th floor. The receptionist greeted us from her white, saucer-like reception desk. Behind her, and also sharing the lobby limelight, stood a 19ft tall totem pole carved from a 100-year old red cedar tree. Dylan and Grace were amazed and ran to the windows to take in the panoramic view of the city. It was stunning!

Galen Weston's team welcomed us warmly. They were very busy making last minute preparations for the book launch the following evening. We were soon joined by Galen Weston himself, who quickly demonstrated he was a man who was very proud of his father's war time activities. I presented him with a DVD that 360 Production had specially produced for me showing some of the key moments of the excavation. He watched the first 5 minutes then turned to his assistant and instructed "We'll need a cinema screen for tomorrow to show this". He explained the running order for the launch and what he wanted me to cover by means of a short talk to his 150 invited guests who included family, friends and Toronto business people.

Next evening, we arrived early for a pre-launch meet and greet with the author and the Westons. The transformation in the reception area was impressive. Framed copies of the local and national Irish papers with our dig headlines were dotted around the walls. Interspersed with these were pictures of Garfield Weston along with some of his famous war time quotes.

Several large monitors ran slideshows of pictures of the Spitfire excavation. At one end of the room a very large cinema screen was set up ready to broadcast the short DVD of the dig highlights. Waiters floated around offering wine and nibbles to the guests.

A contemporary metal staircase linked both floors. On a small landing, halfway up, a lectern had been set up. Galen Weston asked that I speak after the author had officially launched his book. After Professor Vance had said his piece, Galen Weston spoke for a few minutes about his surprise and delight that, at the same time this book was being prepared for launch, he had received news that I had successfully dug the first Weston presentation aircraft out of a bog. He called me up to speak and then, for good measure, invited the rest of my family up to the lectern. I whispered to Andree that now she would have to look really interested. Conscious that this event was someone else's book launch, I spoke for a few minutes about how the dig came about. I read excerpts from a letter the Wolfe family sent over to thank everyone involved in anyway with the dig. I also apologised, as requested on behalf of the Wolfe family, for what their father did to the Weston Spitfire. A round of applause followed and I stepped away from the lectern. Job done I thought!

Galen Weston was having none of it. "Now tell us about who the Eagles were and what they were doing in the RAF before America entered the war" he requested. Without having anything prepared, I gave a brief potted history on the Eagles, their contribution to the war effort and Bud's later career after his release from internment. I invited everyone to enjoy the dig DVD that was to play later on during dinner and that was me done for the night. It was a great evening! We met many interesting people, particularly representatives from the Canadian War Museum who were interested in obtaining some pieces of P8074 for display.

Highlight of the night was the sight of a man striding towards us with his hand outstretched. "I recognise Northern Ireland accents" he exclaimed shaking our hands enthusiastically. "How long are you in town for? – Have you seen Niagara Falls yet? – have you any free days and I'll take you?" He introduced himself as Paddy Carson – the brother of the legendary

Northern Ireland comedian Frank Carson who sadly passed away during the writing of this book. Andree and I exchanged looks. It was that old P8074 surreal thing again. He took us for a grand tour and was the perfect host. We rounded off our stay doing a live TV interview on the CBC news channel. "Do many people watch this programme?" I asked, as a technical person fiddled with an ear piece in my ear. "About 10 million most nights" she whispered and left me alone on my seat. I have no idea what I talked about! We returned home and I thought that, apart from mounting some form of exhibition in a few months time and enjoying the series when it aired next year, all the adventures were over. I considered my days of ringing producer John and stressing him out with yet another revelation had passed.

However there was to follow a twist in the tale that none of us imagined possible. The key ingredients for this unbelievable event were a classic design that hadn't changed since 1919, a skilled Army Ordnance team and a large tank of compressed air.

CHAPTER 11

"Stand By, Firing…Now!"

All 6 Brownings machine guns were now in the capable hands of the Defence Forces Ordnance Corps in Custume Barracks in Athlone, who were going to give them a thorough clean and remove their firing mechanisms. They would be collected in due course, brought to Derry and put on display where hopefully, visitors would be rightly impressed by their condition after a 350mph vertical dive into a mountain bog from 4000ft. I anticipated the display would effectively mark the end of the entire project and I didn't foresee any further revelations in advance of the display. I should have realised never to assume anything in relation to P8074.

So it was early July, when the Ordnance Corps contacted me and, if you pardon the pun, dropped a bombshell in relation to the condition of the 6 Brownings. Captain Lambe explained his team had stripped all the weapons down to their component parts to wash away the mud and peat before bathing them in oil. 5 of them he said were 'almost perfect' with only very slight bends in their barrels. Corrosion was almost non existent and overall he described these weapons as being in excellent condition. Then, after a long pause, he came on to the remaining weapon. After the previous excellent report on the other 5 I fully expected, given the law of averages, that this weapon would be somewhat more battered. I really didn't expect him to proceed to tell me it was 'potentially fully functioning.'

I appreciated it was going to sound like a stupid question to ask what his definition of 'potentially fully functioning' meant, when applied to a war time machine gun that had been driven vertically 16ft into the mountainside after a high speed crash, but I asked it anyway. He admitted the Ordnance Corps technicians were as stunned as I sounded. This one gun he explained was perfect, immaculate in fact, and his armourers intended, subject to my approval, to try firing it. Of all the various revelations connected to the P8074 story, and there had been many contenders during this adventure, this truly was my 'fall off the seat' moment. There were, he added, a few necessary internal checks they had to run to prepare the weapon for firing, but in relation to the weapon itself, there was nothing that needed replacing. This particular gun was going to be fired with the original firing mechanism that was in it when it was retrieved from deep beneath the bog. We agreed to keep this very hush-hush as potentially, subject to tests, the firing may not happen. But if it did happen, well it was going to be nothing short of incredible!

I undertook some research to see if anything similar had ever been managed before. The French authorities in 1981 had apparently managed to get a weapon firing from a Spitfire that had belly landed on a French beach during WW2. In July 1992, a group of Americans retrieved one P-38 Lightning fighter aircraft from deep beneath the ice of Greenland. It had forced landed together with 5 other Lightnings and 2 B-17 Flying Fortress bombers in July 1942 having run out of fuel during a severe Arctic blizzard. All the aircraft were subsequently buried beneath 50 years of snow and ice. They managed to get one of the Lightning's 20mm cannon to fire one round when it was brought to the surface.

The difference between these firings and our gun was that the other weapons involved had been relatively protected from damage when these aircraft had been skilfully 'belly landed' while under a degree of controlled and powered flight. Effectively, they had been gently lowered, within reason, onto the ground during these landings. However our guns had been driven deep into the peat after a high speed vertical crash. If the Armourers could get this gun to fire after this, it was a testament to their skill, the original Browning design and the quality of war time manufacturing at BSA.

While I sat on this information, the relevant firearms authorities in the North and the South had both agreed that decommissioning would not be a fitting end to these historic weapons. This was well received by all including the Armourers who, I was told, had grown quite attached to their war time 'brood'. Decommissioning, they told me later would have been a desecration of these weapons given their impressive condition.

A few weeks later, Lt Col Dave Sexton from Custume Barracks got in touch to say things were progressing well and they had sourced a set of inspection gauges necessary for calibrating things internally before the gun was fired. They hoped to record the firing for posterity and make the footage available to us. With my excitement levels mounting it was time, yet again, to phone producer John and gently break the news to him that there was another twist in the tale. I think that of all the prolonged silences and 'robust expressions of surprise' that emanated from John during the course of this project, this outburst was the most enjoyable. Flustered and incredulous would probably be the best description. As a producer he knew this was a once in a lifetime possibility and not surprisingly we both felt that if the Defence Forces could get the gun to fire we should try to arrange a trip to their range to film a second firing for the series. As was now customary, more minutes were going to have to be allocated to the P8074 segment of episode 1, giving John more editing headaches.

Filming a second firing was of course predicated on the permission and agreement of the Defence Forces. It was quickly agreed that if the gun should test fire successfully, then a repeat performance would be arranged for the benefit of the Dig WW2 cameras. I could only imagine the public reaction to this. The potential viewing figures were likely to go ballistic. It would make tremendous press for the Ordnance team and the Defence Forces in general. All parties agreed a coordinated release of the story between the BBC and the Defence Force Press Office. This would include a BBC webpage story with links to the earlier excavation and a short video clip of the firing. Given the uniqueness of what was being proposed, we realised that this was going to be a major media event and could even surpass the dig reaction. All John and I could do now was sit and wait and hope that the gun fired when the Army took it to the range. It was an agonising wait.

The wait explosively ended at the start of September. An otherwise dull day at work was transformed by the arrival of an email from Lt Col Sexton. It simply stated they had taken the Spitfire Browning to the range that morning and it had successfully fired on the first attempt for each of the following:
- 5 rounds in single shot using modern .303 ammunition;
- 2 x 5 round bursts using modern ammunition; and

- 2 rounds in single shot using ammunition recovered from the bog. One misfired and incredibly one functioned!

All firings were conducted using the metal disintegrating links taken from the bog. These interlocking clips hold the single bullets together to form a belt of ammunition. In case I still didn't believe him a video clip was being emailed to me shortly. 'Play it loud' was his advice. And I did. The silence in the office was broken by a voice shouting "Standby, firing…now!" followed by the most beautiful noise you could imagine. It was a cross between a tear, a rip and a burp. It was the spitting of fire. This sound, frozen in time for 70 years, was the noise of the Battle of Britain emanating from a very historic and unique weapon. Heads looked up from their office computers and turned in my direction and then went back to their work. My work colleagues had no idea what they had just heard, or its significance. I was happy for it to stay that way until the firing, if it happened, went public.

It was the enthusiasm and curiosity of the Ordnance technicians that really impressed me. Not satisfied with cleaning the guns and holding them until I could collect them, they had the urge to see if they could get one of them to fire. It must be an ordnance thing! Prior to all this firing excitement, I had polished up a large gear cog from the engine and mounted it on a wooden plinth to give to the team as a small token of my appreciation for all that they had done. Now I seriously had to reconsider my level of giving. Just what do you give soldiers as a 'Thank You' for working such a miracle? The answer was simple – two Spitfire machine guns. They were delighted with the offer and gratefully accepted. They proposed to put them on display in the Officers Mess at the Barracks. Well that's what they told me, but knowing these guys, they probably have these guns firing as well.

We managed to finalise a date in early November that suited all concerned and the 360 team. Presenter Dan Snow, my son Dylan and I met up at a hotel in Athlone. Lt Col Sexton joined us for an hour later on in the evening to introduce himself and run through what the Ordnance team had organised for the next day and safety guidelines in terms of filming the event.

Next morning, after John and Dan filmed a few pieces to camera in the surrounding Athlone countryside, we drove up to the imposing front gates of Custume Barracks which occupies a large area of the west bank of the River Shannon. The historic Barracks today serve as the headquarters of the Western Command of the Irish Defence Forces. We had tea in the Officers Mess during which I caught Dan teaching Dylan how to stuff chocolate biscuits into his pockets to eat later on. As honorary Officers, I told them their conduct was unbecoming. Sniggering followed and they were instantly reduced in rank for the rest of the day.

After tea we were escorted up to see Colonel Aherne who wanted to meet the team behind the excavation. As the Barrack's Commander he gave us a warm welcome and an excellent military history of the Barracks and Athlone town. He was delighted at how the excavation had evolved to give his team the chance to show their skills. John outlined to him the joint media approach we were proposing. I had been liaising with the BBC web site designers in the days running up to the firing to ensure the technical accuracy of the story and the graphics and I knew they were very excited about the story should this second firing go to plan. I just hoped that on the day we released the story on an unsuspecting world nothing else exciting on the news front happened. Dylan and I presented the Colonel with a polished Merlin engine cog as a token of our thanks. He in turn surprised us by proudly handing out copies of a commemorative colour booklet his Ordnance team had produced recording their participation in the dig. They contained details on Bud, the guns and photographs of what they had achieved on the range on their first firing day. After a few more official photographs for the military album, we went to meet the Ordnance Corps technicians who had breathed life back into one of these 70 year old guns.

All the remaining Brownings were sitting out on a bench in the Armoury. The transformation in their appearance since I had last held them was remarkable. They were spotlessly clean and possessed a sinister type of beauty despite their dainty size. The soldiers had one of the weapons stripped down and they showed us the relatively simple construction methods and the ease with which they could be re-assembled. Another pointed out the minor imperfections in some of the other barrels that prevented these weapons from joining the other on the range. They had done an impressive job and several bottles of whiskey were deservedly presented to them and added to the Armoury drinks cabinet for later enjoyment. After more filming we left in a convoy of trucks and wagons and headed to the range.

The range was a bitterly cold place. Situated at the side of the Shannon, it was reached through a series of anonymous looking farm gates. Each gate bore a successively more threatening warning notice. A few tough looking cows scowled as we gently nudged past them in our vehicles and drove up to the firing point where the rest of the Ordnance team were waiting for us. The range was flat with a large earth bank at one end to stop the bullets. In front of this was a robust metal frame on which wooden targets could be hoisted up and down remotely. At set distances back from the targets there were low grassy banks and concrete slit trenches from which the Defence Forces could take up positions to fire.

Like the star of the show, our Browning sat on a tripod approximately 100 meters from the target. Immediately behind it was one of the trenches. The barrel was restricted within a metal hoop to ensure it couldn't move from that position when firing. A pneumatic hose ran from the gun down to a large compressed air tank which nestled safely in the trench. The air was needed to power the firing mechanism. On the Spitfire this would have been delivered from two air bottles stored directly behind the pilot's seat. This compressed air supply, the length of new hose and modern .303 ammunition were the only concessions used for the attempt. Otherwise the gun, including its internal firing mechanism, was unaltered. It was exactly the same gun that had been pulled from the bog.

Before we started firing, the Defence Forces demonstrated that an Army does indeed march on its stomach. They quickly put up a large field tent and several cooks arrived and set up a first class mobile canteen, dishing out steaming plates of curry. Suitably warmed and full, it was soon time for the main event. The Range Safety Officer set out in no uncertain terms what was expected from us and the protocol to be religiously followed each time the gun was to be fired. Dan got kitted up in full body armour and strode off the trench from where he would throw the lever that would fire the machine gun. The cameras were set up behind the gun to catch the noise, smoke and falling spent ammunition. Enviously, Dylan and I watched from much further back. It all went silent. Then Dan called out "Stand by, firing… now!" and a short burst ripped the afternoon stillness. There was cheering and waving from the trench and Dan turned and delivered a suitably exhilarated piece to camera. Further firings followed using successively longer belts of ammunition. With the longer bursts there was dramatic smoke and flame. You could watch the target flinching under the impact and see the soil spurting up behind it as the rounds buried themselves deep into the bank. It was a fascinating spectacle to watch and a truly unique moment to witness.

Just when I thought that was the show over, Lt Col Sexton walked back from the firing point to where Dylan and I had been watching all the action. He brought with him a very long belt of ammunition. It held 47 rounds of bright, brassy ammunition. "Come on" he said to me "you got us into this mess, you can have the honour of firing the last burst". Stunned at this news as I did not expect to get the opportunity to fire the gun, I quickly got kitted up in the fading November evening light and walked down to the trench and crouched behind the Browning. Lt Col Sexton brought Dylan a bit closer to get a better view. In the seconds before firing, I thought back to the magical moments when Grace and I found the crash location, when the magnetometer shrieked when it detected the exact crash site and the marvellous finds on the excavation day. Could I possibly have imagined that three months later, after handing over those peat encrusted guns, that I would be sitting in a trench in Athlone about to fire one of them? It was the stuff of dreams.

The Range Safety Officer handed over control of the firing sequence to me. I took a deep breath and in a very poor attempt at a calm voice I called out "Standby…Firing…Now!" and the gun sang and then fell silent. That was it. That was the last time that gun was ever going to fire. 47 smoking cartridge cases lay scattered around the tripod feet, like flowers on a fresh grave, marking its passing. It was quite a bittersweet moment for me. Dylan walked over as I clambered out of the trench and we shared a happy hug. I told him that the gun would never do what it had been designed to do ever again. What a life it had experienced! It had soared through the skies in a Spitfire's wing, chased and shot down one Luftwaffe bomber, survived a high speed crash and then, after an interval of 70 years, it still had the ability to fire. It registered with Dylan that this was a special moment. Something you could not learn from a school book. He walked over to the Browning as it sat silently on its tripod and rested his hand on top of the still warm breech. In his best Farmer Hoggett impression from the film Babe, he simply said "That'll do Gun, that'll do". We all knew exactly what he meant and what we had witnessed. Now we needed to share it with the world.

The unsuspecting public didn't have long to wait. The web site article had been written in advance and was quickly updated in the light of the successful firing. A short video in the article featured a clip of the gun in action and some tempting highlights from the excavation day. It was unleashed on the BBC website on the 10th November. I had hoped that this would be a quiet news day and our story would feature strongly. Sadly some wannabe pop star from a talent show decided this would also be a great day to get kicked out of the competition for participating in dodgy activities. We anticipated the customary media frenzy and public hysteria over his departure and realised we were going to have some stiff competition throughout the day.

Regular updates were posted to all involved from the web team to keep us informed of the impact our story was having. By early afternoon the story had already received the same number of hits as the excavation had registered over the entire day. It was running neck and neck with the outpouring of grief over the X-Factor story. I couldn't believe our Browning was proving so popular. Stunned emails whizzed between the Defences Forces, producer John, Dan and myself as we watched the story snowball. The true enjoyment though was not derived from the viewing figures, but from the comments being posted on the BBC website. Very bizarre cross sections of the public were soon leaving their thoughts for all to read. We had praise, allegations it was a faked stunt and continuing debate over WW2 internment in Ireland. Perhaps the most satisfying posting was a wonderfully composed eulogy from an American praising the genius of the gun's designer.

Writing on the 11th November – Veterans Day in the USA – he invited readers to:

Take a vet to lunch today and buy them a beer and thank them for their service. Hoist another one to Mr Browning who kept so many of them alive and gave them a lot of the tools they needed to keep us all free.

The figures showed no sign of stopping and the story topped the 'Most Read Feature' on the website throughout the rest of the day. Next day, the BBC web team released their final figures. It was phenomenal. 1,008,329 individuals had viewed the page. By far the most read feature on the day. And the programme still hadn't aired yet! All involved in the programme were delighted; the BBC NI executives were reported to be 'over the moon'. It all bode well for a successful series.

Although it was great to see the firing grabbing the public's imagination, I really wasn't that interested in the viewing statistics or target audiences. It was a relevant side show, but now I had to re-focus on what was truly important to me, which had always been Bud's story. While all the preparations were being made for the gun firing, I had been making preliminary arrangements for a fitting display of P8074 in the Workhouse Museum in Derry. I was overjoyed to receive an email from Bud's daughters, Betty and Barbara, informing me that they and 12 other members of the extended Wolfe family had booked their tickets and were coming to Ireland. Everything I had done up to this point was going to pale into insignificance in the weeks ahead. I had just over three weeks to arrange a display in conjunction with the Museum Department. I had to arrange a suitable itinerary and launch event that would sensitively cater for what would truly be a very emotional visit. It was time to unveil P8074 to the public in all her battered glory.

CHAPTER 12

A Gathering of Wolves

As the end of the year approached, discussions began in earnest with Derry City Council in relation to arranging a launch for the exhibition. Betty and Barbara had emailed a few weeks previously to say that they and 12 other members of the extended family had booked their tickets as part of a grand tour of Ireland and were intending to come to Derry for 4 days towards the end of November. It wouldn't be your average city break. Parts of the trip were likely to attract keen media interest and leave the family feeling emotionally battered and bruised. It was incumbent on the Council and myself to prepare a respectful itinerary and a display that was worthy of the city and befitting of Bud's memory and war time service at Eglinton.

One date was clearly going to be very poignant for the family during their stay. The 30th November 2011 would be the 70th anniversary of the crash and I knew I had to get all the family out to the crash site on this day. So it was time to get myself back into organising mode again and start preparing lists. Just when my wife thought I had been successfully rehabilitated into family life again, I was away again, organising what became known as the 'Gathering of Wolves'. It was a torturously tight deadline with only 3 weeks to go.

The immediate priority was to agree a realistic itinerary with the staff in the Museum. It quickly became apparent that the Workhouse Museum in the Waterside area of Derry was the only museum that could accommodate the 650kg engine. The available space in the Workhouse meant that only a fraction of all the recovered pieces would go on display. In due course, it is intended that the proposed new Maritime museum at Ebrington in Derry will proudly host all of P8074 in one display. We developed a list of things to do. On paper it appeared daunting and I won't pretend it all went like clockwork. The small team in the museum and I rallied together with the limited resources at our disposal and soon had somehow worked our way through a lengthy list. How? – I don't know, it was all a bit of a blur. There were interpretative display boards to design and create; organising the logistics of getting the engine on display as well as designing and building a large metal stand to hold it. Don't forget catering, managing invites for 80 guests, writing speeches for the Mayor and organising the media and press releases and you will soon appreciate the definition of the word 'frantic'.

For the 30th, the City of Derry Airport team proposed an afternoon unveiling of a plaque that I was having designed and made in England thanks to the generous donation from Galen Weston. In addition, they would take the family out to the now abandoned WW2 runway that Bud flew from during his brief stay in Eglinton. This left the morning clear to take the 14 members of the party out to Moneydarragh for a visit to the crash site, exactly 70 years to the day that it happened. If everything went to plan and the weather played ball, we could gather in silence at 12 30pm, the exact time the crash occurred. My father, a Church of Ireland minister, had recently come out of retirement to take on in a part time role, a group of parishes on the Inishowen peninsula. Fate again had decreed that one of these parishes included the townland of Moneydarragh. He kindly offered to take a short service of commemoration at the site. While deeply appreciative of this offer, I had serious concerns about what a 500m walk through a bog was going to do to his white clerical robes!

The Mayor of Derry, Alderman Maurice Devenney, was a strong supporter of the project and he was very keen to formally welcome Betty and Barbara to the city. His office made preparations for a civic reception and a Mayoral tour for them around the Guildhall, after which they would be driven in the Mayor's official car to the Workhouse museum to launch the exhibition. He also made a donation towards the daughters travel costs from the Mayoral funds. The city was pulling out all the stops for our guests to ensure they enjoyed a welcoming and respectful visit. Derry was going to demonstrate that all involved in the exhibition appreciated them making the effort to travel from America.

Around this time, I received an email from Bud's elder sister, Theaople who was 96 and living in a nursing home in California. She was bitterly disappointed at not being able to travel with the rest of the group as she was recovering from a broken hip. Theo, as she is known, sent us her best wishes and thanks for all the team had done. She and many WW2 aviators who reside in her nursing home had been following our progress on their computers, cheering us on from afar. I got the impression, that in the absence of her recent accident, she would have been leading the Wolfe family onto the aircraft and over to Derry. To console her, I sent her a small package containing a few small pieces of her brother's aircraft. In her reply, she added that she had become quite a local celebrity in her home, with many of the residents dropping by for the latest update. She is very proud of Bud's career and her touching letters and emails also reveal a very sprightly mind and a great sense of humour – characteristics, I am told, Bud shared.

The family visit was keenly anticipated by the local press who had followed the story since its breaking days. They were naturally keen to get an opportunity to speak to Betty and Barbara and attend the various events. Some of the events were clearly going to be emotionally hard for the daughters and this aspect of the trip was given considerable thought. In the end I felt compelled to email them and ask them their feelings on the matter. They responded that they too had been thinking about this. It wasn't so much the press attention that concerned them. Their main worry was how they were going to articulate what the sudden television spotlight, on a relatively unknown part of their father's life, meant to them as a family and their memories of him. Did it close the war time chapter of his life or pose more questions? Either way, they stated they were happy to meet the media and attempt to put into words how they felt and to have the opportunity to thank all those who had respectfully handled their father's aircraft and his personal effects.

The day finally arrived when the extended Wolfe family arrived in Derry. They emailed to say they had all made it to the hotel and were looking forward to meeting me that evening. They had landed in Dublin the previous week and immediately began a cultural tour of some of the tourist sites around Ireland. Some headed to the landscape of the west coast, taking in the Curragh camp on the way. Some shopped and a few were rumoured to have visited 'just a few' pubs in Dublin to attend to some compulsory Guinness sampling.

I must admit I was very nervous as I parked the car in the hotel car park and took the lift to reception where I had arranged to meet the group. Despite exchanging emails constantly for 8 months, I had only spoken to them briefly on the phone. 10 months ago I barely knew the pilot's name. Now, in a few minutes time, I was going to meet his daughters in person and I didn't know what to do. Was it handshakes or was it a hug? Would there be tears and not knowing what to say? Too late, the lift doors opened and I stepped out into the foyer and there before me were Pilot Officer Roland 'Bud' Wolfe's two daughters and an assortment of husbands, nephews and great nieces and nephews. A span of ages and all united to learn about Bud.

Immediately after all the introductions, it was time for Betty and Barbara to have a quiet few moments in a conference room where the Council Museum staff had laid out Bud's flying helmet, oxygen mask and items recovered from his first–aid kit. These had been brought out of protective storage in the Museum where they were being prepared for preservation and accordingly they could not sit out under the room lights for too long. Betty and Barbara slowly moved forward from the group who respectfully held back to allow them a few silent minutes with their own thoughts at the table. Wearing cotton gloves and with trembling hands, they reverently picked up their father's flying helmet and marvelled at its condition. Slowly moving down the table, they inspected his oxygen mask and held the long lengths of Sutton harness that had restrained him in the cockpit until he decided it was time to go and unbuckled them. Betty commented how the 70 years seemed to disappear when holding these harness straps. "My father tore these straps away as he baled out and now 70 years later, we are holding them. The time in between just melts away" she said quietly. As many tears flowed, I quickly appreciated how articulate these two ladies were and how they could beautifully express their feelings.

As the Museum staff packed away these fragile items, I felt I had to apologise to the group for such an emotional start to their visit. I thought this occasion was the most appropriate to view their father's items. Apart from the 360 camera crew who remained discretely in the background during the viewing, this was a family moment. They all agreed it was never going to be easy, but now having quietly viewed Bud's personal effects and shed the first of many tears, they felt they had the beginnings of the emotional strength needed to deal with the days ahead. This was good to hear because the next day was the 30th November 2011. Exactly 70 years to the day of the crash, there would again be a Wolfe presence on the Glenshinny mountain.

The 30th November, after two weeks of almost non-stop rain, was dry but with a biting wind blowing. We arrived at the site shortly before noon and suitably wrapped and insulated we carefully picked our way across the knee deep heather and peaty puddles down to the spot where P8074 had buried itself. All the visitors were immediately captivated by the wildness of the location. Some tried to comprehend what it had been like all those years ago as the silence of the moor was torn asunder by the wailing scream of the Merlin engine in its plummeting death throes. Buffeted by the wind, the group huddled together solemnly while my father delivered a short service of thanks and prayers for Bud and all his war time colleagues. He included a short prayer from a war time prayer book for the Armed Services I had picked up years ago from a second hand bookshop. In the minutes leading up to 12 30pm, he read the following prayer for the Air Force:

Almighty God, who makest the clouds thy chariot and walkest upon the wings of the wind; have mercy, we beseech thee, on our airmen, and when they are amidst the clouds and wonder of the skies, give unto them the assurance of thy protection, that they may do their duty with prudence and with fearlessness, confident that in life or in death the eternal God is their refuge, and underneath are the everlasting arms; through Jesus Christ our Lord. Amen.

Having read this passage, he looked at his watch and announced it was exactly 12 30pm on the 30th November 2011. 70 years to the very minute since the crash occurred. There was a short silence during which quiet tears were whisked away from many faces and blown across the moor. After we had finished, Betty and Barbara presented me with a plaque they had discretely smuggled down to the crash site. It was a most unexpected and appreciated gift, made more significant to have received it from them at the site on the 70th anniversary. The common feeling amongst the visitors as we headed back to the cars was not one of sadness, but of a warm enrichment, an inner strength with which they had all been imbued by visiting the site.

After a quick stop to defrost with tea and coffee at a local hotel, we moved on to the City of Derry Airport, where a plaque commemorating Bud, 133 (Eagle) Squadron RAF and Eglinton resident, the late Nat McGlinchey was unveiled by Betty and the Mayor. It comprised two floating perspex panels, telling the story of P8074, suspended in front of a brushed metal background engraved with a soaring Spitfire. Barbara unveiled a display case that held the complete tail wheel of P8074, small fragments of aluminium and pieces of the propeller and copies of historical documents and photos relating to Bud's career. While this was ongoing, passengers arriving for flights stopped to watch and enquire what was happening and warm applause greeted the unveilings.

There then followed another one of those surreal P8074 moments as we were ushered onto a coach and driven, in the early evening gloom, down the now abandoned war time runway. It is a rather uneasy feeling to drive down an airport runway, abandoned or not, in a small coach. It takes a bit of getting used to! At the far end the party stepped out into a howling gale and stood for a few minutes to take in this historic environment that their father would have known well. The silhouette of the Donegal hills in the distance behind Lough Foyle revealed just how close Bud came to nursing his ailing aircraft back to base. As the wind did its best to blow hats and hairstyles across the airfield, we posed for a group photo on the runway, before seeking the sanctuary of the coach. The chatter on the way back to the terminal echoed the earlier thoughts and feelings coming off the moor. In following Bud's footsteps and visiting these significant locations they felt in a sense they were reinforcing their proud memories of him and his war time service. Their spirits were upbeat. They had returned to these locations and in visiting had simply said "Dad, we are proud of what you did".

Early next morning, I took Barbara to the BBC Radio Foyle studios to pre-record an interview with Mark Patterson for his afternoon programme. It was clear from his questions that he appreciated such a visit to Derry, to acquaint themselves with a part of their father's life that they knew little about, was going to be emotionally painful. It was genuinely very tough to sit beside Barbara and listen to her talk of the frustration and sometimes even anger she felt at her father's reluctance to discuss his war time memories, and he had served in three - WW2, Korea and Vietnam. Even though Barbara had also had a successful career in the United States Air Force, and accordingly shared a common bond with her father, he would not reminisce with his family. This trip, she said, opened up some boxes that she thought were closed in relation to remembering and grieving for her father. It was a mentally tough interview and rather red eyed we left the studio to collect Betty and meet the Mayor at the Guildhall for a guided tour.

The Mayor's civic welcome was a welcome antidote to the earlier challenging interview. Mayor Devenney was an excellent host and officially welcomed Betty and Barbara to the city. After presenting them with Derry City Council plaques, he toured them around the Guildhall pointing out the historical nooks and crannies of this impressive building. Both ladies were very impressed and appreciative of this formal welcome, and even more so when they were escorted to the Mayor's official car to drive over to the Workhouse Museum. Waiting there were nearly 80 people representing all those who had, in any way, assisted in this project. It was time to launch the public exhibition and tell the story of Spitfire P8074.

At the museum, all those who had participated and had given freely of their time and expertise to enable it to happen, mingled upstairs among the artefacts on display waiting the Guests of Honour. Downstairs in the reception area, the press gathered near the Merlin engine that had powered P8074 on its last flight. It was a very proud moment for me to introduce Betty and Barbara to this engine which immediately grabbed their attention. Its sheer bulk and its incredible preservation make it a very tactile, touchable object and soon the ladies were added to the long list of people who had simply walked up to it and given it a silent stroke.

The Mayor led the ladies upstairs to meet the assembled crowd for what was scheduled to be a short series of speeches. In a long room, lined on both side by the invited guests, press and the 360 Production camera crew, the Mayor was called forward to say a few words by Roisin Doherty, Head of the Council's Heritage and Museum Service who was the MC for the launch event. In formally welcoming them to the city, he hoped that they had enjoyed themselves, despite their hectic schedule and that they would take back fond memories of the city and pass them on to their friends and family in America.

Then Betty stood up and delivered a most poignant address. Her carefully delivered words, interspersed with quotes from the poetry of Raymond Carver (Waiting) and Seamus Heaney (Postscript) soon silenced the gathered crowd in that room as she spoke of the close bond between the members of the 133 Squadron and the deep and abiding love those men had for their aircraft. 'Compose yourself Jonny!' I kept repeating to myself, as a slightly teary Roisin then asked Barbara to say a few words.

Barbara is also a skilled orator. Her emotional speech soon had hankies appearing in many hands. She recounted her father's career and how overwhelming it had been to stand on the runway, looking down the centre white line and seeing the countryside that would have been a familiar sight to him. She finished by acknowledging the dig had allowed the family another opportunity to honour those who served. For the work done and the hospitality shown she added "We thank you from open hearts."

I took a deep breathe and stood up to make a speech from a series of notes I had typed up the previous evening. In an attempt to pull myself together, I stared down the room, avoiding any direct eye contact with the invited guests. Unfortunately all I could see was dabbing tissues and streaming mascara. I lasted to the second bullet point on my page when I had to stop. Suddenly all the emotion I had stored during the last year decided this was the ideal time to escape. Doing my best 'stiff upper lip', I lurched from bullet point to bullet point, frequently pausing as waves of emotions spilled over. I had written a special line of thanks to my long suffering wife for all she had endured. I recall squeaking my way through that section. To make matters worse, as I was stumbling over these lines, the camera crew swivelled round to catch Andree in mid sob. Never have I been more relieved to say 'Thank you' and take a step back from a crowd. I felt physically and mentally shredded and it was a few minutes before I was fit for a conversation with anyone. Betty, Barbara and I embraced and jokingly agreed there and then never to do this again!

The rest of the launch was a blur of meeting all those who had been involved throughout the project and thanking them. It was also the only opportunity for those who had participated on the dig day to meet those people who had worked behind the scenes. Brothers Danny and Martin Kearney reminisced about the dig with the City of Derry Airport management. The Northern Ireland Office officials who worked on the machine gun paperwork marvelled with the Queen's University survey team about the state of preservation of the gun on display.

The story and exhibition of P8074 had been emotionally launched in the city where it was based during WW2 by the two daughters of the pilot. It couldn't have been any more fitting. It was no less than this historic aircraft and Bud Wolfe deserved.

That evening, the visitors kindly took my family out to dinner. Over a very relaxing meal we recalled the events of the last 72 hours into which, we all agreed, we had seemingly packed a lifetime of emotional experiences. Later back at the hotel, we enjoyed a very happy parting. Having participated in such a personal journey with Betty, Barbara and the extended family over the last year we knew we would keep in touch. They left Derry with a better understanding of a previously lesser known part of their father's war time career and a firm appreciation that a city, many thousands of miles away, had taken their story to its heart.

As I drove out of the hotel car park and into the quiet Derry streets, I cast my mind back over an incredibly momentous year. I was still amazed that this search that started with such a low expectation of success and that was only supposed to be a 5 minute filler in the series, had become this big international story. I smiled as I recalled that everything that had transpired during the year was the result of my daughter Grace and her fondness for chocolate buttons. That request for a packet of sweets back in January started a series of events that culminated, almost a year later, with Bud's family and relatives travelling on an emotional journey that enabled them to trace their father's footsteps from Derry to the Curragh.

But without a doubt, the overriding reason why P8074 was such a successful project was the way in which complete strangers came together to share their time, equipment and expertise to assist in what I often jokingly referred to as my noble quest. Bewitched by the word Spitfire and Bud's story, individuals, organisations and Government Departments took that leap of faith and swelled the ranks of a small team whose only vision was to recover and display P8074 to the best of their ability and ensure that Bud's story was faithfully told.

Did we do it right? Those with the greatest emotional stake in the project certainly thought so. Letters of sincere appreciation followed in the days after the dig from Betty, Barbara and Bud's elder sister Theo. We were acutely aware that in digging this site and telling their father's story we were likely to generate many heart wrenching moments for the family.

As I journeyed home, I wondered what Bud would have made of it all. His daughters consistently spoke of a quiet man who loved his aircraft but remained firmly tight lipped about his war time career. They wrote in an open letter to the team:

"We know that Bud Wolfe did not attribute political or even 'historical' significance to his military career, nor even his life experiences. However, he loved flying and appreciated the Spitfire above all other aircraft he flew.
We feel certain that he would be stoically ecstatic to heft the tail wheel, lay hands on the propeller, tinker with the Rolls Royce Merlin engine and maybe slip on the flying gear when no one was watching."

It sounded like Bud would have stayed in the background during all our events, uncomfortable to be in the media spotlight. It would have been reward enough to have caught a wistful smile from the great man as he stood in quiet contemplation beside the Merlin. No other words would have been necessary.

What if Bud Wolfe and Garfield Weston looked down on the day of the dig and recognized in the team some of their own respective characters – an enduring passion for Spitfires and a determination to succeed when attempting something new. Perhaps, just perhaps, Garfield Weston, having viewed our efforts in undertaking this unique project, would say of everyone involved in his rousing 1940 tones:

'When it came to the battle, they did not fail! They did not fail! They did not fail!'